Y0-BEM-390

# 2011 Edition

## Carson City • Carson Valley • Reno/Sparks
## Lake Tahoe/Truckee

**LOCAL'S DISCOUNT GUIDE, LLC**

1528 Hwy 395, Suite 210

Gardnerville, NV 89410

(775) 783-9119 Fax (775) 783-9476

info@localsdiscountguide.com

# INDEX BY CITY AND CATEGORY

# INDEX BY CITY AND CATEGORY

# INDEX BY CITY AND CATEGORY

# INDEX BY CITY AND CATEGORY

# INDEX BY CITY AND CATEGORY

**ALPHABETICAL LISTING**
**IN REAR OF BOOK**

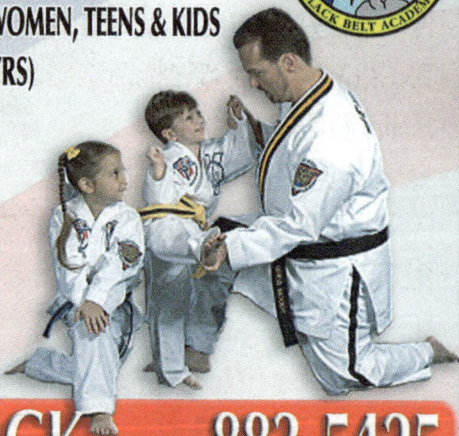

12

# Naan & Kabab etc.

This healthy Mediterranean 3-course meal is served in a cozy, friendly, fine-dining atmosphere.

Our friendly, experienced wait staff cater to our customers with prompt, attentive service.

**Chef Maurice Welcomes You!**

MEDITERRANEAN STEAK PLATTER

CHICKEN KOOBEDEH

• FINE DINING • TAKE OUT • CATERING
• MEETINGS • PARTIES • BELLY DANCING

Visit us at **www.naanandkabab.com**.
Take our virtual tour.
Read our customer testimonials.
Please leave your comments on **yelp.com**.
Become a fan on **facebook**.

**775-825-3113**
2740 S. Virginia St., Reno, NV 89502
Across from the Peppermill

**Menu on reverse**

# Naan & Kabab etc.

## Includes:
### NAAN, HOUSE SALAD, CHOICE OF ONE ENTRÉE OR SANDWICH, AND DESSERT

### Salad

Crispy hearts of romaine, ripe roma tomatoes, cucumber, and sweet red onions mixed with extra virgin olive oil, and 10-year aged sweet balsamic vinegar.

### Entrée Choices

**Veggie Kabab** Marinated seasonal vegetables roasted on an open fire.
**Kabab Koobedeh** Mixture of ground beef (filet, sirloin, chuck, lamb), onion pulp, saffron, and turmeric, hand-formed on skewer and roasted on an open fire.
**Chicken Koobedeh** Ground chicken breast and thigh, with onion pulp, saffron, and turmeric, hand-formed on skewer and roasted on an open fire.
**Falafel Sandwich** Traditionally-made with garbanzo beans, spices, our famous tasty, creamy tahini sauce, and garnishes, served in a grilled pita wrap.
**Mediterranean Steak Platter** 8-oz marinated "chuck tender" cut steaks served with marinated vegetables roasted on an open fire and basmati rice.
**Veggie Combo** Dolmades, falafel, our famous homemade hummus, and baba ganoush served with grilled pita bread and special naan.
**Gyro Sandwich** Roasted tender pieces of tri-tip in house special marinade, wrapped in grilled pita bread, with tzatziki, lettuce, and garnish.
**Koobedeh Sandwich** Mixture of ground beef (filet, sirloin, chuck, lamb) marinated with onion pulp, saffron, and turmeric, served with tzatziki sauce and garnish, wrapped in a grilled pita.
**3/4-lb Mediterranean Burger** Mixture of ground beef (filet, sirloin, chuck, lamb) with onion pulp, saffron, and turmeric, served with tzatziki sauce and garnish on a grilled onion roll.
**Salad Platter & Bowl of Soup** Homemade chicken "medi-strone", with nine fresh vegetables and pasta shells, flavored with saffron, garlic, basil, and spices. (Vegetarian medi-strone or lentil soup available.)

### Dessert

Awesome Dude **Baklava a la Mode**
Saffron ice cream, pistachios, vanilla, rose water, and pieces of cream topped with baklava chunks.

# Teen Life / My Life Workbook

- *Intro*
- *Meet "Stix"*
- *Who am I?*
- *Communication*
- *Peer Pressure*
- *Boundaries*
- *Feelings and Emotions*
- *Abuse and Addiction*
- *Stop the Violence*
- *Daily Inventory*
- *Closing Letter*

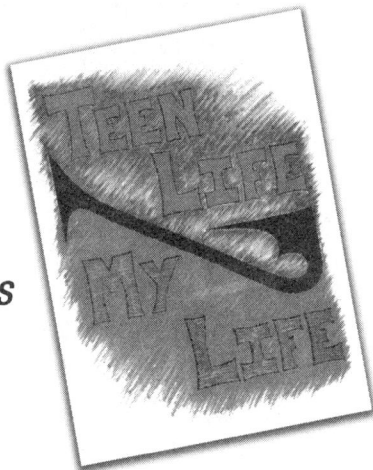

A useful tool to help improve any teen's life. This workbook will help teens make good and healthy decisions!

To order: 775-291-4559

Mention Local's Discount Guide
Pay only $7.50
(25% of the cover price of $10)

# STOP AND PRAY

STOP AND PRAY

**Wholesale / Retail Merchandise**
**Positive Impact Products**

**T-Shirts • Posters • Coffee Mugs • Water Bottles**
**Hats • Pencils & Pens • Wrist Bands**

**Special orders are no problem**
**Customize your organization**

*Mention Local's Discount Guide and*
*receive 50% off retail prices*

**Order by phone or online**
**1.775.291.4559**
**www.stopandpraystuff.com**

# Carson City

## Complimentary Chilled Prawns

with Zesty Cocktail Sauce & Lemon Caper Aioli
or Baked Brie in Phyllo Cups for
Any Catering Over $300.00
### OR *10% Off Your Entire Bill*

Expires December 31, 2011

**Bella Vïta**

"The Good Life"
Cheese · Fine Food · Catering

**Bella Vïta Catering**
"The Good Life"

Distinctive catering for
all occasions.
From an intimate evening for 2
to a festive party for 500.

Bella Vita
specializes in all the little details
that will make your event
truly successful.

**Hot & cold Appetizers** (Bruschetta, Assorted Crostini, Pesto Torta,
Prawn Butter served with Baguettes)

**Soup & Salads** (Greek, Caesar, Potato, Pasta, etc)

**Sandwiches** (Meatloaf; Chicken, Egg and Tuna Salad; Turkey, etc)

**Entrees** (Seafood Paella, Fettucini Alfredo, Tri Tip served w/Tri Sauces,
Chicken Chardonnay, etc)

**Sushi** (Classic raw, cooked classic rolls, customer rolls, etc)

**Desserts** (Mini Cream Puffs, Brownies, Cheesecakes, Mousse, etc)

This is just a sampling of some of the delicious menu items we
offer, we are always happy to work with you on custom menus!

775-783-9475 phone / 775-783-9476 fax

# www.bellavitacateringtgl.com

# Canyon Creek
## GRILL & BAR

US 50 | S. CARBON ST | SNYDER AVE | US 395 | JACKS VALLEY RD | 939 MICA DRIVE

20

**RED'S OLD 395 Grill**

## Buy 1 Lunch Item
## Get 2nd Item FREE
**Equal or lesser value. Up to $15.00.**
**Dine in only. With purchase of two beverages.**
**Not good with any other offer.**

Expires December 31, 2011

*1055 S. Carson St., Carson City 89701 • 775-887-0395*

**1055 S. Carson St., Carson City 89701 • 775-887-0395**

# RED'S OLD 395 Grill

# FREE Appetizer
## with Purchase of
## Two Dinner Entrees
### Not to exceed $10.99. Dine in only.
### Not good with any other offer

Expires December 31, 2011

23

**The Branding Iron**
cafe & steakhouse

**The ChuckWagon**

Pioneer Crossing Casino - Dayton
4 Pine Cone Road
Dayton, Nevada 89403
Ph: (775) 246-6600

Pioneer Crossing Casino - Fernley
1705 Highway 50A
Fernley, Nevada 89408
Ph: (775) 585-4444

**PIONEER CROSSING**
CASINO•RESTAURANT•SALOON
www.pioneercrossingcasino.com

**"You're More Than a Guest, You're a Friend & Neighbor!"**

**2 for 1 at the Branding Iron Cafe in Dayton or the Chuckwagon Restaurant in Fernley**

Dine-in and regular menu items only. Daily specials not included.
Please present coupon to server at time of order. Expires December 31, 2011

**LOCAL'S DISCOUNT GUIDE**

**San Marcos Grill**

San Marcos Grill
260 E. Winnie Ln
Carson City, NV 89706
775.882.9797

Offer validity is governed by the Rules of Use and excludes defined holidays. Offers are not valid with other discount offers unless specified. Coupons void if purchased, sold or bartered. Discounts exclude tax, tip and/or alcohol, where applicable.

**LOCAL'S DISCOUNT GUIDE**

**THE SPOKE Bar & Grill**

The Spoke
3198 N. Deer Run Rd.
Carson City, NV 89701
775.887.1117

Offer validity is governed by the Rules of Use and excludes defined holidays. Offers are not valid with other discount offers unless specified. Coupons void if purchased, sold or bartered. Discounts exclude tax, tip and/or alcohol, where applicable.

* All offers of 2 for 1 or Buy 1 Get 1 are good on equal or lesser valued items only.

**LOCAL'S DISCOUNT GUIDE**

# Buy 1 Entree, Get 2nd 50% Off

Sixteen years in the same location.

Best tasting breakfast in Carson City.

**Mom & Pops DINER**

Expires December 31, 2011

---

* All offers of 2 for 1 or Buy 1 Get 1 are good on equal or lesser valued items only.

**LOCAL'S DISCOUNT GUIDE**

# Buy 1 Entree, Get 2nd 50% Off

New Restaurant.
Located on east side of Carson Mall.
Good Food, Tropical Atmosphere,
Tropical Drinks, Beer & Wine.

Owned by Mom & Pops Diner.

**PARADISE COVE Cafe**

Expires December 31, 2011

**Local's Discount Guide**

# Mom & Pops DINER

Mom & Pops Diner
224 S. Carson St.
Carson City, NV 89705
775.884.4411

**Local's Discount Guide**

PARADISE COVE Cafe

Paradise Cove Cafe
1200 S. Stewart St.
Carson City, NV 89705
775.841.1199

# DINING

29

# V&T COFFEE COMPANY

## Try our famous
## White Locomocha or
## The Mother Lode!

Located next
to Raley's at
3667 S. Carson St.
Carson City, NV
775-841-1229

**LOCAL'S DISCOUNT GUIDE**

# Garibaldi's
### Ristorante Italiano
## (775) 884-4574

Garibaldi's
307 N. Carson St.
Carson City, NV 89701
775.884.4574

**"We Toss 'em, They're Awesome"**
**PIZZA FACTORY**®

**LARGE 1- 3 TOPPING**
# PIZZA
# $10⁰⁰

**WITH THIS CARD.**

Not valid with any other offer. Limit one
coupon per person per visit. Exp. 12-31-11

# FAMILY MEAL DEAL
# $25⁹⁹

XL 1 OR 2 Topping Pizza, 12
Chicken Wings, Bread Stix &
2 Liter Soda

Not valid with any other offer. Limit one
coupon per person per visit. Exp. 12-31-11

**Open Sun - Thurs 11 am - 9 pm ● Fri - Sat 11 am - 10pm**

---

**"We Toss 'em, They're Awesome"**
**PIZZA FACTORY**®

**LARGE 1- 3 TOPPING**
# PIZZA
# $10⁰⁰

**WITH THIS CARD.**

Not valid with any other offer. Limit one
coupon per person per visit. Exp. 12-31-11

# FAMILY MEAL DEAL
# $25⁹⁹

XL 1 OR 2 Topping Pizza, 12
Chicken Wings, Bread Stix &
2 Liter Soda

Not valid with any other offer. Limit one
coupon per person per visit. Exp. 12-31-11

**Open Sun - Thurs 11 am - 9 pm ● Fri - Sat 11 am - 10pm**

## Local's Discount Guide

"We Toss 'em, They're Awesome"

**PIZZA FACTORY®**

**CARSON CITY**
**775-882-9800**
**WE DELIVER**
3120 HWY 50 EAST #3
ADDITIONAL CHARGES MY APPLY
GOOD @ CARSON LOCATION ONLY

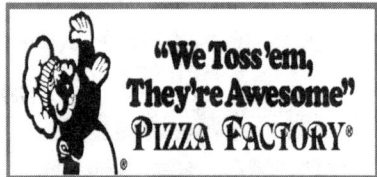

"We Toss 'em, They're Awesome"

**PIZZA FACTORY®**

**CARSON CITY**
**775-882-9800**
**WE DELIVER**
3120 HWY 50 EAST #3
ADDITIONAL CHARGES MY APPLY
GOOD @ CARSON LOCATION ONLY

Offer validity is governed by the Rules of Use and excludes defined holidays. Offers are not valid with other discount offers unless specified. Coupons void if purchased, sold or bartered. Discounts exclude tax, tip and/or alcohol, where applicable.

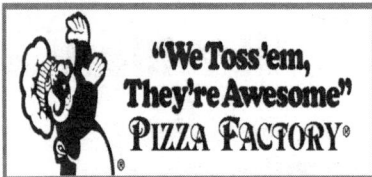

## Local's Discount Guide

"We Toss 'em, They're Awesome"

**PIZZA FACTORY®**

**CARSON CITY**
**775-882-9800**
**WE DELIVER**
3120 HWY 50 EAST #3
ADDITIONAL CHARGES MY APPLY
GOOD @ CARSON LOCATION ONLY

"We Toss 'em, They're Awesome"

**PIZZA FACTORY®**

**CARSON CITY**
**775-882-9800**
**WE DELIVER**
3120 HWY 50 EAST #3
ADDITIONAL CHARGES MY APPLY
GOOD @ CARSON LOCATION ONLY

Offer validity is governed by the Rules of Use and excludes defined holidays. Offers are not valid with other discount offers unless specified. Coupons void if purchased, sold or bartered. Discounts exclude tax, tip and/or alcohol, where applicable.

**LOCAL'S DISCOUNT GUIDE**

# Buy 1 Entree, Get 2nd
# Entree 1/2 Off

"We've Got the Whole Enchilada!"
246-TACO

## Compadres Mexican Food

165 Pike Street • Old Town Dayton
Open for Lunch & Dinner
11:30am to 9 pm
Serving Dayton for Over 12 Years

Expires December 31, 2011

---

* All offers of 2 for 1 or Buy 1 Get 1 are good on equal or lesser valued items only.

**LOCAL'S DISCOUNT GUIDE**

# Buy 1 Entree, Get 2nd
# Entree 1/2 Off

"We've Got the Whole Enchilada!"
246-TACO

## Compadres Mexican Food

165 Pike Street • Old Town Dayton
Open for Lunch & Dinner
11:30am to 9 pm
Serving Dayton for Over 12 Years

Expires December 31, 2011

**LOCAL'S DISCOUNT GUIDE**

**Compadres Mexican**
165 Pike St
Dayton, NV 89403
775.246.8226

**LOCAL'S DISCOUNT GUIDE**

**Compadres Mexican**
165 Pike St
Dayton, NV 89403
775.246.8226

# COMSTOCK ENERGY.com
## 775-883-6409

Receive a free upgrade
with the purchase of a new stove or fireplace
Up to $300.00 Value

Expires December 31, 2011

# Sierra Hearth & Home
## Sierra Closet & Blind

**See us for:**
- Solatube
- Fireplaces
- Stoves
  wood • gas • pellet
- Window Coverings
  shutters • drapes
- Closet & Garage Systems
- Fulline Showroom
- CA & NV Licensed
- Sales • Service
- Installations
- Design Consults

- Store Hours:
  Mon-Thurs 9-5
  Fri 9-4:30
  Sat 10-2

**Carson Quail Center**
2350 S. Carson Street, Suite #1
Carson City, NV 89701

Phone: (775) 882-1522
www.sierrahearth.com
**Free Estimates**

# 10% Off

**☼ SOLATUBE.**
Innovation in Daylighting™

**Sierra Hearth & Home**
Sierra Closet & Blind

Expires December 31, 2011

36

# Candle Scent-Sations & Gifts

775-841-0444

1958 Highway 50 East. Carson City, Nevada 89701

## YES, WE ARE STILL OPEN. NEW LOCATION
## LARGER STORE WITH MANY NEW ITEMS

PROFILE PICTURE FRAMES (NEW), AMIA HAND PAINTED GLASS, GRANNY GOODSCENTS SOY CANDLES, ALOHA BAY PALM CANDLES, XTREAM CARVED CANDLES (NEW), MASSAGE CANDLES, PAINTED PONIES, AYE CHIHUAHUAS, CALL OF THE WILD WOLVES, SALT & PEPPER SHAKERS, MONEY JARS (NEW), 3D BOOK MARKS (NEW), MAGNETIC JEWELRY (NEW), SILVER JEWELRY (NEW), TREE FREE NOTE CARDS AND BAGS, WIND CHIMES, OVER 200 TARTS WARMERS (ALSO ELECTRIC) AND 180 TARTS, KEY RINGS, TIME & AGAIN BODY PRODUCTS

### PLUS MANY MORE CANDLE ACCESSORIES AND GIFT ITEMS

*Larger selection of Fantasy & Fairy figurines from Amy Brown, Nene Thomas, Jessica Galbreth, Jasmine-Beckett also Tinkerbell, Pegasus, Unicorns, Dragons and Gargoyles*

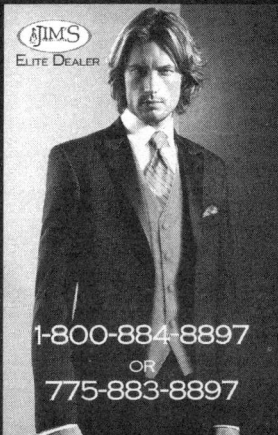

40

# Thank you for your continued support of the Carson City School District.

www.carsoncityschools.com

## LOCAL'S DISCOUNT GUIDE

We offer a whimsical and eclectic selection of gifts. Thoughtful gifts for all seasons and reasons. Voted Carson City's Best Gift Store!

HOURS:
Tu-Fri 10 am-5:30 pm,
Sat 10 am-4:30 pm
Also open EVERYDAY between Thanksgiving and Christmas!

Expires December 31, 2011

# 20% Off
## any 1 item

### the
# PURPLE AVOCADO
### gifts of an extraordinary nature

thepurpleavocado.com

---

## LOCAL'S DISCOUNT GUIDE

Play It Again Sports
911 Topsy Ln Suite #226 A
Carson City, NV 89705
775.267.3390

HOURS:
M-F 10 am-8 pm
Sat 9 am-7 pm
Sun 10 am-6 pm

Expires December 31, 2011

# 20% Off
## Your Next Purchase
### Offer excludes sale and consigned items.

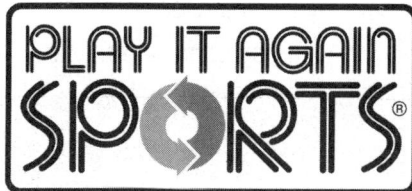

# PLAY IT AGAIN
# SPORTS®

**LOCAL'S DISCOUNT GUIDE**

the
**PURPLE AVOCADO**
gifts of an extraordinary nature

The Purple Avocado
904 N. Curry St
Carson City, NV 89703
775.883.6233

**LOCAL'S DISCOUNT GUIDE**

**PLAY IT AGAIN SPORTS®**

Play It Again Sports
911 Topsy Lane Suite 226A
Carson City, NV 89705
775.267.3390

**LOCAL'S DISCOUNT GUIDE**

**ALOHA**
Discount Wine & Liquors
4555 So. Carson St
(Hwy 395) Carson City
775-882-5544

FREE
BOTTLE OF
WINE
WITH ANY
$25
PURCHASE

This coupon is good for 10 visits

| 1 | 2 | 3 | 4 | 5 | 6 | 7 | 8 | 9 | 10 |

Expires December 31, 2011

---

# $5 off
## a $30 minimum purchase

**GROCERY OUTLET** bargain market

1831 N. Carson
Carson City, NV 89701
775-882-6199
7 am - 8 pm Every Day!

Valid at Carson City Grocery Outlet only. One coupon per person. Minimum purchase excludes dairy & alcohol. No cash value. Not valid with any other offer.

0  00000 64578  2

Expires December 31, 2011

**LOCAL'S
DISCOUNT
GUIDE**

**ALOHA**
Discount Wine & Liquors

Aloha Liquors
4555 S. Carson St.
Carson City, NV 89701
775.882.5544

**LOCAL'S
DISCOUNT
GUIDE**

**GROCERYOUTLET**
*bargain market*®

## Shop us First. Save the Most.

1831 N. Carson • Carson City, NV 89701
775-882-6199 • 7am - 8pm every day!

*See other side for special coupon!*

47

**LOCAL'S DISCOUNT GUIDE**

SIERRA LE BONE

Sierra Le Bone
3817 S. Carson St.
Carson City, NV 89701
775.885.2663

**LOCAL'S DISCOUNT GUIDE**

# TILE OUTLET
## ALWAYS IN STOCK ®
TILE • GRANITE • MARBLE • TRAVERTINE • SLATE • GLASS
• MEDALLIONS • PRE-FAB GRANITE • *AND MUCH MORE!*

**$500 OFF** on back

**Local's Discount Guide**

# 20% Off
## Hardware
## with Door Purchase

Carson Door
4300 Ryan Way
Carson City, NV 89706
775.841.3667

HOURS: Mon-Fri 7 am-5 pm

**CarsonDoor**
841-DOOR

Expires December 31, 2011

**Local's Discount Guide**

# Spin
## our Wheel of Fortune
### for a free gift or store discount

Rocking & Rolling - Carson City's
most unique gift shop. Rocks,
crystals, fossils, books, jewelry,
railroad and western souvenirs,
and "Made in Nevada" products.

Located at
402 N. Curry St. Carson City
775.267.5144
Hours: Wed-Sat 11-5

ROCKING AND ROLLING

**LOCAL'S DISCOUNT GUIDE**

**CARSON DOOR**
841-DOOR

Carson Door
4300 Ryan Way
Carson City, NV 89706
775.841.3667

ROCKING AND ROLLING
FURNITURE OF MINING AND RAILROAD COLLECTIBLES

*Browsers*
*Welcome*

*Buyers*
*Adored*

Rocking & Rolling
402 N. Curry St.
Carson City, NV
775.267.5144

51

## CARSON CITY

Processing Plant:
Bobby Page's Dry Cleaners
1310 S. Stewart St.
(775) 882-6262
*Same day service offered*

Winnie Center Dry Cleaners
156 W. Winnie Lane
(775) 882-9285

Bobby Page's Dry Cleaners
3173 Hwy 50 East
(775) 884-4844
Open Every Day 7 am-9 pm
Next to Wash Tubs Coin Laundry
Carson's Newest 72 Washer Store

## GARDNERVILLE

Bobby Page's Dry Cleaners
1516 Hwy 395
Haas Center
(775) 782-2911

## Bobby Page's (Roundhill)

Zephyr Cove, NV
Next to Safeway
(775) 588-8066

**Bobby Page's DRY CLEANERS & Shirt Laundry**

## Our #1 Goal is to Earn Your Business

# Quality Auto

# 10% Off
## Any Service Over $100

Expires December 31, 2011

# CAPITOL OVERHEAD DOOR

"Since 1973"

## SALES • SERVICE • INSTALLATION
## RESIDENTIAL & COMMERCIAL
## STEEL • WOOD • INSULATED GARAGE DOORS

SPRING REPLACEMENT - QUICK SERVICE

**Custom Wood & Carriage House Doors**

**AMARR • Windsor • R&S**

**Cookson • Bonanza • Porvene**

**Automatic Operators**

**Licensed • Bonded • Insured**

GENIE PRO
CHAMBERLAIN

BBB
Northern Nevada, Inc.

LiftMaster
PROFESSIONAL

## (775) 882-0812

301 HOT SPRINGS RD • CARSON CITY • FAX 775-882-0893

EMERGENCY CELL
(775) 560-4687

# SERVICE

**LOCAL'S DISCOUNT GUIDE**

**Jigsaw Automotive**

Jigsaw Automotive
301 Hot Springs Rd #7
Carson City, NV 89706
775.883.5447

**LOCAL'S DISCOUNT GUIDE**

## "Service you can count on"

* Outboard / 4 Stroke
* Inboard
* Stern Drive
* Tune-Ups/Lube/Oil
* Boating Supplies & Accessories

Since 1994

* Spring Get Ready
* Winterizing
* Shrink Wrap
* Storage

CARSON TAHOE MARINE

carsontahoemarine@att.net

## LOCAL'S DISCOUNT GUIDE

# AVADA INSURANCE

Avada Insurance
301 E. William St.
Carson City, NV 89701
775.887.9800

Offer validity is governed by the Rules of Use and excludes defined holidays. Offers are not valid with other discount offers unless specified. Coupons void if purchased, sold or bartered. Discounts exclude tax, tip and/or alcohol, where applicable.

## LOCAL'S DISCOUNT GUIDE

# AVADA NOTARY

Avada Insurance
301 E. William St.
Carson City, NV 89701
775.887.9800

Offer validity is governed by the Rules of Use and excludes defined holidays. Offers are not valid with other discount offers unless specified. Coupons void if purchased, sold or bartered. Discounts exclude tax, tip and/or alcohol, where applicable.

**LOCAL'S DISCOUNT GUIDE**

Contreras Auto Body
3031 N. Deer Run Rd.
Carson City, NV 89701
775.884.2332

**LOCAL'S DISCOUNT GUIDE**

## TIRES FOR YOU

Tires For You
5460 Hwy 50 E.
Carson City, NV 89701
775.882.4850

**LOCAL'S DISCOUNT GUIDE**

## Accurate Mobile Locksmith
24 hour locksmith service -- Licensed, Bonded & Insured

**Accurate Mobile Locksmith**
**P.O. Box 840**
**Minden, NV 89423**
**775.265.7444**
**883.8444**

**LOCAL'S DISCOUNT GUIDE**

## *Custom Firearms & Gunsmithing*

**Custom Firearms**
**10198 Hwy 50 E**
**Moundhouse, NV 89706**
**246.2333**

# HandJive

*A Full Service Salon*

## 50% Off
### any single service

Expires December 31, 2011

# HandJive

*A Full Service Salon*

- Hair - Chemical Services - Cut & Style
- Manicures, Artificial Nails, Pedicures
- Facial Treatments
- Lash Tinting
- Brow Waxing
- Permanent Makeup
- Tanning

Call for Appointment, Walk-Ins Welcome

## Get Your Groove On!

### 10196 Hwy 50 East Carson City NV 89706
### 775-246-5335

63

Change Your Body. Change Your Life.™

**3790 HWY 395 #402, CARSON CITY, NV 89705 • 775.267.1700**

# NO START UP FEES!!

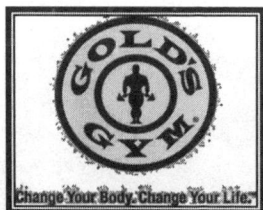

*Come in and give us a try!!*
*What's the worse that can happen?*
*You lose a few pounds!*
*We are next to Trader Joe's\**

# No START UP FEES!!

Change Your Body. Change Your Life.™

Expires December 31, 2011          HOURS: Mon-Fri 4:30 am-9 pm    Sat/Sun 6 am-8 pm

**LOCAL'S DISCOUNT GUIDE**

# 20% Off
## Total Purchase

GNC
933 Topsy Ln. #421
Carson City, NV 89701
775.885.0559

HOURS:
Mon-Fri 10 am-6:30 pm
Sat 10 am-6 pm
Sun 12-5 pm

**GNC** Live Well.

Expires December 31, 2011

---

**LOCAL'S DISCOUNT GUIDE**

# 10% Off Retail
# $5 Off Service
## with select stylist

Re~Nu Salon
1894 Hwy 50 E. #9
Carson City, NV 89701
775.883.2515

Open Mon-Sat at 10 am

*RE~NU*
salon & spa

Expires December 31, 2011

**LOCAL'S DISCOUNT GUIDE**

**GNC** Live Well.

GNC
933 Topsy Ln. #421
Carson City, NV 89701
775.885.0559

**LOCAL'S DISCOUNT GUIDE**

*RE~NU*
salon & spa

Re~Nu Salon
1894 Hwy 50 E. #9
Carson City, NV 89701
775.883.2515

# Thank you for your continued support of the Carson City School District.

www.carsoncityschools.com

*Offering Pottery Painting, Glass Fusing, Clay Sculpting and MORE!*

*We also host Birthday Parties, Kids Camps, Workshops, Field Trips....*

**Walk-ins Welcome EVERYDAY!**

Located in Carson City in the Best Buy shopping center!
775-267-3366
Follow us on Facebook!
www.MakeitYoursFiredArts.com
MakeitYoursFiredArts@live.com

# Make it Yours!

## Fired Arts Studio

HOURS:
Monday-Friday 11am-7pm
Saturday 10am-8pm
Sunday 11am-4pm
(We close an hour early if no one is in the shop!)

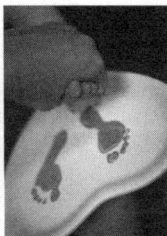

# Free Studio Fee
## (A $7 Value)

Studio Fee includes: the firing of your projects, use of our tools and help from our friendly, qualified staff!
*(not valid with any other offer or event special)*

Expires December 31, 2011

## Make it Yours!

### Fired Arts Studio

68

**702 Skate & Snowboard Shop**
911 Topsy Ln. Ste. 234 (Next to Best Buy)
Carson City, NV 89423
(775) 267-3831

Open 7 Days: Sales - Rentals (Snowboards) - Repairs

## 15% Off
Any Regularly Priced Skateboard
Shoes, Tee's, and Hoody's

## Free Black Grip Tape
with Skateboard Deck Purchase

Expires December 31, 2011

70

NEVADA DEPARTMENT of

CULTURAL AFFAIRS

## NEXT STOP, NEVADA
### CIRCA 1900

The rich railroading heritage of northern Nevada lives on at the Nevada State Railroad Museum in Carson City.

An extraordinary collection of railroad equipment, artifacts and related exhibits portray how the railroad transformed a hostile frontier territory into an essential contributor to the growing nation in the late 19th and early 20th centuries. Visitors can learn about the important role played by the world-famous Virginia & Truckee Railroad in obtaining Nevada's distinction as the "Silver State."

Enjoy rides aboard restored V&T railcars or the 1926 Edwards motorcar on weekends from May through September. Once a year, the Inyo is fired up and brought out on the tracks as part of the museum's annual Independence Day celebration.

**NEVADA STATE RAILROAD MUSEUM, CARSON CITY – 775.687.6953**
2180 South Carson Street Carson City, Nevada 89701

## NevadaCulture.org

DIVISION OF MUSEUMS AND HISTORY – NEVADA DEPARTMENT OF CULTURAL AFFAIRS

nevăda

# Carson Valley

# *Antoci's Restaurant*
# NEW MENU
Come see what you've been missing!
**Authentic Italian & Southern Cuisine.** Something for everyone!

**Tues** ~ Pasta Night (pick your own pasta) starting at $11
**Wed** ~ Prime Rib Night $15 (includes salad)
**Thurs** ~ No Corkage Night (1 per table)
**Thurs, Fri, Sat** nightly specials

*Perfect for any occasion. Call about our group and party*
*accomodations and reservations at 782-6645.*
*www.genoalakes.com (Click on Antoci's)*

**Bring this coupon in and receive a**
## FREE Appetizer
**with the purchase of (2) or more entrees**
One Per Table. Not valid with any other coupon or promotional discount.

*Antoci's Restaurant*

Not valid Tues-Weds or w/ any other discount or promotional ad

Expires December 31, 2011

**Buy One Specialty Coffee Beverage**
# Get 2nd Specialty Coffee
## at 50% Off

**G**ENOA
CANDY & COFFEE CO.

Expires December 31, 2011

**G**ENOA
CANDY & COFFEE CO.

We are located in the Genoa Square offering Fresh Roasted USDA Certified Organic Coffee along with our scrumptious Pastries, Muffins, Scones, Cookies. We offer a variety of over 200 candies from homemade fudge to historical favorites and sugar-free. We also have award-winning truffles and other confectionary delights your imagination desires. We are very proud to serve Authentic Italian Gelato & Sorbetto.

**2292 MAIN STREET, SWEET #3 - GENOA, NEVADA 89411**
**2600 SNYDER LANE, SUITE C - CARSON CITY, NV 89701**

## P.O. BOX 789 (775) 782-8500
### www.genoacandyandcoffee.com
*Located in the Genoa Country Inn Hotel*

**BREAKFAST SERVED DAILY**
**7:30 AM TO 11:30 AM**
**CREPES, WAFFLES, QUICHE**
**BISCUITS & SAUSAGE GRAVY**
**STOP BY FOR A FREE SAMPLE**
**ORGANIC FRESH ROASTED COFFEE**
**& OUR HOMEMADE FUDGE**
TUESDAY-FRIDAY 7:30 AM-4:30 PM
SATURDAY 7:30 AM-4 PM
SUNDAY 7:30 AM-2 PM
CLOSED ON MONDAYS UNLESS ROASTING COFFEE

# Round Table PIZZA

**CARSON CITY**
3325 Retail Dr.
In College Parkway
Shopping Center
**884-8080**

961 Topsy Ln.
Next to Best Buy
**267-9577**

**DAYTON**
9 Retail Rd.
In Smith's
Shopping Center
**246-1199**

**GARDNERVILLE**
1327 Highway 395 N.
At Waterloo Lane in Carson
Valley Shopping Center
**783-9777**

# WE DELIVER!!

## All You Can Eat Lunch Buffet
### $6.99
Daily from 11:00am-2:00pm

## Family Night Buffet
| Adults | Kids 4-10 | 3 & Under |
|--------|-----------|-----------|
| $6.99  | $3.99     | FREE      |

Tuesday Nights 5pm-8pm

## CREATE YOUR OWN
Any Large
1-Topping **$12.00**
Pizza

Dine-In, Carry-Out, or Delivery

Expires December 31, 2011

## CLASSIC SPECIALTIES
Any Large
Classic Specialty **$16.00**
Pizza

Dine-In, Carry-Out, or Delivery

Expires December 31, 2011

# THE WILD HORSE

## PIZZA BAR GRILL
### MINDEN, NEVADA

# Buy One, Get One
# 50% Off
## (Value Up to $6.00)

# THE WILD HORSE

Come see why we're consistently voted the **BEST BURGER** in Carson Valley as well as one of the **BEST PLACES TO DINE!**

## PIZZA BAR GRILL
### MINDEN, NEVADA

1679 Hwy 395 N. #C
(775) 782-7208
(775) 782-2508 (fax)

Great Burgers • Sandwiches • Salads • Pizza • Kid's Menu
Happy Hour • 7 TV's • NFL Sunday Ticket • Video Poker

Open Mon-Fri from 11:00 am, Sat-Sun from 11:30 am
Call ahead for quick take-out!
All major credit cards accepted.

To satisfy your cowboy hunger

# Cowboy's Café

Serving Breakfast & Lunch Open 6am–2pm Closed Mondays

1679 A Hwy 395 • Minden
782-8800

Voted Best Breakfast

# FREE Coffee w/ Meal
**with this coupon only**
Expires December 31, 2011

## Complimentary Chilled Prawns
with Zesty Cocktail Sauce & Lemon Caper Aioli
or Baked Brie in Phyllo Cups for
Any Catering Over $300.00
## OR 10% Off Your Entire Bill

**Bella Vita**
*"The Good Life"*
Cheese · Fine Food · Catering

Expires December 31, 2011

**Bella Vita Catering**
*"The Good Life"*

Distinctive catering for
all occasions,
From an intimate evening for 2
to a festive party for 500.

Bella Vita
specializes in all the little details
that will make your event
truly successful.

**Hot & Cold Appetizers** (Bruschetta, Assorted Crostini, Pesto Torta, Prawn Butter served with Baguettes)

**Soup & Salads** (Greek, Caesar, Potato, Pasta, etc)

**Sandwiches** (Meatloaf; Chicken, Egg and Tuna Salad; Turkey, etc)

**Entrees** (Seafood Paella, Fettucini Alfredo, Tri Tip served w/Tri Sauces, Chicken Chardonnay, etc)

**Sushi** (Classic raw, cooked classic rolls, customer rolls, etc)

**Desserts** (Mini Cream Puffs, Brownies, Cheesecakes, Mousse, etc)

This is just a sampling of some of the delicious menu items we offer, we are always happy to work with you on custom menus!

**775-783-9475 phone / 775-783-9476 fax**

# www.bellavitacateringtgl.com

# *Tahoe Ridge* WINERY ®

## Marketplace & Bistro

**Come in to Tahoe Ridge Winery, Marketplace & Bistro** and Get Half Off of the 2nd Entree Menu Changes All the Time and We Have Great Specials Nightly *Hope to See You Soon!*

**50% Off Second Entree** of equal or lesser value Not good for parties over six.

Expires December 31, 2011

*Tahoe Ridge* WINERY ®

Marketplace & Bistro

**Saletti's**
RESTAURANT & BAR

# Saletti's
## RESTAURANT & BAR
*Minden, Nevada*

**Happy Hour in our Lounge 4-6 daily**
**Early Dining Menu 4-6 daily**

Our lunch menu features Freshly Tossed and Chopped Salads, Mouth-Watering Soups, Sandwiches, Italian Offerings, and Daily Specials.

Dinner Selections: Certified Angus Beef, Fresh Fish, Seafood, Wild Game, and Specialty Pastas.

All desserts made on premise by Faith Saletti and Michelle Lindsey.

**1623 Hwy 395, Minden, NV**
**782.2500**
**Family-Owned and Operated**
**Lunch M-F 11-2**
**Dinner Daily 4 pm**

PIZZA FACTORY

# We Toss 'Em They're Awesome!

## Under New Ownership

Stop by to meet the new owners
and use these Awesome Deals!

1758 Highway 395
Minden
783-0800
We Deliver

Open 7 Days
Sun-Thurs 11 am-9 pm
Fri-Sat 11 am-10 pm

| COUPON | COUPON | COUPON | COUPON |
|---|---|---|---|
| Large 2 Topping $10 Out the Door | Order 6 Chicken Wings $1 with purchase | Free 1/2 Deli Sandwich with purchase of Any Whole Sandwich | 2 Large 2 Topping $22.00 |
| Expires 12/31/11 | Expires 12/31/11 | Expires 12/31/11 | Expires 12/31/11 |

# Free Dessert
with purchase of
full-size entrée

**or**

# Free Chef's Choice
# Appetizer
with purchase of full-size entrée

Buona Sera Ristorante & Bar • Good for up to 4 people.
Cannot be combined with any other offers.
Cannot be used during certain holidays.

Expires December 31, 2011

# Buona Sera Ristorante & Bar

*Voted Carson Valley's
Best Of #1
Place for Dinner
AND #1
Italian Restaurante*

*Winner of the
Taste of the Towns
for Best Taste and
Best New Discovery*

**1799 B Ironwood Dr.
Minden, NV**
www.buonaseraminden.com
**775-783-3211**

## ASIAN BISTRO

*A local's favorite serving global dishes from Japan, Thailand and the Far East*

**Wasabi's**
Sushi & Asian Bistro

*A full bar with a great selection of Asian beers, sakes, & tropical drinks. Kid's menu & take-out available*

Price Range
$3.75- $23.00

1657 Lucerne St Bldg D Minden, NV  89423   775-783-3210

VISA

### Appetizers

Tempura Shrimp . . . . . . . . . . . . . . . . . . . . . . . . . . . . Served w tempura dipping sauce
Gyozas . . . . . . . . . . . . . . . . . . . . . . . .Oriental dumplings served with ponzu sauce
Asian Egg Rolls  . . . . . . . Stuffed with shrimp, crab, carrots, onions and cream cheese

### Salad

Sunomono Salad  . . . . . . . . . Crisp light cucumber salad sprinkled with sesame seeds
Nando Salad  . . . . . . . . . . . . . . . .Fresh mango, crab, tobiko and shredded lettuce
Far East Chicken Salad . . . . . . Cashews, shallots, water chestnuts and mixed greens
Samurai Beef Salad . . . . . . . .Grilled sirloin steak, fresh greens and chili lime dressing
Seared Tuna Salad . . . . . . . .Fresh grilled tuna, served on cucumber and greed salad

### Soups

Japanese Onion, Miso or Ginger chicken & Coconut Soup

### Noodle & Rice Bowls

Yakimeshi . . . . . . . . . . . . . . . . . . .Fried rice bowls with chicken, pork, beef or shrimp
Phad Thai . . . . . . . . . . . . . . . . . . . . . . . . . . . . . . . . . . . . . . .National Dish of Thailand
Sesame Chicken & Shanghai Noodles . . . . . . . . . .Baby bok choy, garlic and ginger.

### Wasabi's Specialties

Beef or Chicken Teriyaki, Sizzling Malaysian Steak, Curry Pork w/Pineapple,
Shrimp & Vegetable Tempura Platter, Wasabi's Salmon
*lots more!*

## Buy 1 Teppanyaki
### Receive One of Equal or Lesser Value at 50% Off

**Wasabi's** Sushi & Asian Bistro

Expires December 31, 2011

*The perfect choice for any celebration or occasion.*
*Reservations Required*

# TEPPANYAKI

**Wasabi's** Sushi & Asian Bistro

*World Class Teppan Chef will delight in this interactive dining experience.*

*Price Range*
*$19 - $39*
*per person*

1657 Lucerne St Bldg D Minden, NV 89423   775-783-3210

VISA

## Dinner

*Choice of Chicken, Teriyaki Steak, Salmon, New York Steak, Calamari Steak, Shrimp, Scallops, Lobster or Filet Mignon*

All dinners include a choice of Wasabi's House Onion Soup or Miso Soup, Wasabi's Shrimp Appetizer, Asian House Salad, Fried Rice and Tea.

## Wasabi's Combos

*Chicken & Shrimp, New York Steak & Salmon, New York Steak & Shrimp, Teriyaki or New York Steak & Chicken, Seafood Combo – Scallops, Shrimp & Calamari, Filet Mignon & Shrimp or Scallops, Filet Mignon & Lobster Wasabi's Special – New York Steak, Lobster & Shrimp*

## Kid's Menu

*Choice of Chicken, Shrimp or Steak*

Kid's dinners (10 & Under) include shrimp appetizer, vegetables, fried rice and ice cream

Price Range
$3.75- $23.00

## SUSHI BAR

VISA

*Wasabi's*
Sushi & Asian Bistro

The local's
favorite
sushi bar !!

All-You-
Can-Eat or
A La Carte

1657 Lucerne St Bldg D Minden, NV  89423   775-783-3210

### Raw Sushi ~ Cooked Sushi ~ Raw Hand or Long Rolls
### Veggie Hand Rolls ~ Cooked Hand and Long Rolls - Sashimi

Tempura Shrimp . . . . . . . . . . . . . .Tempura Shrimp, spicy crab, avocado, and onions
Playa Blanca . . . . . . . . . . Cooked snapper, cilantro, onions, avocado and spicy sauce
Godzilla . . . . . . . . . . . . . . Salmon, snapper and yellowtail with onions fried in tempura
Tempura Roll . . . . . . . . . . Tempura fried crab, salmon, cream cheese and jalapenos
Peluza . . . . . . . . . . . . . . . . . . . . . Panko crusted fried half roll w/tuna, salmon,
                                                   snapper, crab, cream cheese and onions
No Name . . . . . Tempura shrimp, pecans, cream cheese, avocado and spicy scallops
Pink Lady . . . . . . . . . . . . . . . .Spicy tuna, cucumber w/seared tuna and tobiko on top
Rukky . . . . . . . . . . . . . . Deep fried spicy tuna, salmon, onions and spicy crab on top
Wendy . . . . . . . . . . . . . . . . . . . .Crystal shrimp, avocado, special sauce and onions
Macho . . . . . . . . . .Crystal shrimp, spicy sauce, onions, jalapenos and cream cheese
Tropical . . . . . . . . . .. . . . . . . . . . Tempura shrimp, cream cheese, pecans, tempura
                                                   banana topped with mangos and strawberries,
                                                   drizzled with mango syrup
Caterpillar . . . . . . . . . . . . . . . . . . . . . . . . . . . . . . . . Unagi, crab and avocado on top
Fuji Mountain . . . . . . . . . . . . . .Crystal shrimp, special sauce, tuna salmon, yellowtail
                                                   and avocado on top covered with spicy crab

## TO GO ORDERS WELCOME

### Buy 1 Get 1 Free
### All You Can Eat or Any Roll
### of Equal or Lesser Value

*Wasabi's*
Sushi & Asian Bistro

Expires December 31, 2011

**Buy 1 Regular Hamburger**

# Get One Free

Expires December 31, 2011

## Wolf Creek
## Restaurant/Saloon
### Hours of Operation:

*Winter: Nov 1-Apr 30*
Mon: 11-3 pm
Tues: 11-8 pm
Weds Closed
Thurs: 11-3 pm
Fri 9-9 pm
Sat 8-9 pm
Sun 8-8 pm

**(530) 694.2150**

**14830 St. Hwy 89**
**Markleeville, CA 96120**

*Fine Foods & Spirits*

*Summer: May 1-Oct 31*
Open 7 Days
Mon-Thurs 8-8 pm
Fri-Sun 8-9 pm

# Thank you for your continued support of the Carson City School District.

www.carsoncityschools.com

# Buy 1 Entrée
# Get 2nd Free
**Of equal or lesser value. Present Coupon.**

1665 Lucerne St. Minden, NV 89423
775-782-4300
Reservations not required, but suggested for parties over 8.

Join us for "Open Mic Night"
every Thursday

A cool and contemporary dining area wrapped around a central bar with a diverse menu of both familiar and adventurous fare with a large selection of wines and beverages.

**Get Started** Housemade Potato Chips & Dip, Buffalo Wing Dip w/Tortilla Chips, Field Greens w/Dressing, Hot Artichoke Dip w/Crostini, Buffalo Wings,

**Bar Fare** Swiss or Sharp Cheddar Fondue w/Baguette, Chocolate Fondue w/Fresh Fruit, JD's Curly Prawns, Signature Tacos.

**Entrée Salads** "The Indigo", Grilled Chicken Caesar, Southwest Blackened Salmon, Iceburg Wedge

**Side Kicks** House Fries, Seasonal Fruit, Indigo Potatoes, House Pasta, Veggies of the Day, Macaroni and Three Cheeses.

**Main Event** Sirloin Burgers, Tri Tip Dip w/Au Jus, Seared Prawns Over Pasta, Drunken Short Ribs, Chicken Douglas (house specialty).

\* \* \* \* Live music or DJ provides entertainment on weekends \* \* \* \*

A fabulous place for Sunday Brunch that includes Filet, Crab and Vegetarian Benedicts; Crepes; Omelets ; Biscuits & Gravy as well as other standard menu items

# The New Rancho Grande

Restaurant & Cantina
Home of The Best Margaritas in Town !!!!!!

Fresh Mexican Food & Grill
An Authentic Mexican Dining Experience

1404 Hwy 395 Main Street est. 1998
To Go Tel # 775 782 6145

**LOCAL'S DISCOUNT GUIDE**

# Buy Super Burrito
### and receive
# Free Soft or Crispy Taco

A family owned and operated business that has been serving delicious, homemade Mexican food for over 17 years. We use only fresh, wholesome ingredients in our flavorful dishes without the shortcuts of lard or MSG. Our walk-up-and-order restaurants offer extensive menu choices, a wonderful salsa and pepper bar and fast service.

Dine in or take out.

Expires December 31, 2011

## SUPER BURRITO

---

**LOCAL'S DISCOUNT GUIDE**

# 2 For 1
## or 50% Off Pastry
### Sugarplum Bakery

Specialty Cakes! Baking up goodies for you! Across from Wasabi's Sushi Bar in the Minden Village Quiche, Soups, Salads, Panini. All Made to Order Call for our Full Service Catering!

783-8828

Open Tues-Sat
8 am-6 pm,
Sun 8 am-3 pm

Expires December 31, 2011

## Sugarplum
### Bakery & Treats
*"A Delicious Adventure"*

**LOCAL'S DISCOUNT GUIDE**

## SUPER BURRITO

Super Burrito
1670 Hwy 395
Minden, NV 89423
775.230.5075

**LOCAL'S DISCOUNT GUIDE**

## Sugarplum
### Bakery & Treats
*"A Delicious Adventure"*

Sugarplum Bakery
1649 Lucerne St. Suite C
Minden, NV 89423
775.783.8828

LOCAL'S DISCOUNT GUIDE

88 CUPS

88 Cups Coffee & Tea
1663 Lucerne #B
Minden, NV 89423
775.783.0688

Offer validity is governed by the Rules of Use and excludes defined holidays. Offers are not valid with other discount offers unless specified. Coupons void if purchased, sold or bartered. Discounts exclude tax, tip and/or alcohol, where applicable.

LOCAL'S DISCOUNT GUIDE

TWO GUYS from ITALY

Two Guys from Italy
1488 Hwy 395
Gardnerville, NV
775.782.4897

Offer validity is governed by the Rules of Use and excludes defined holidays. Offers are not valid with other discount offers unless specified. Coupons void if purchased, sold or bartered. Discounts exclude tax, tip and/or alcohol, where applicable.

## LOCAL'S DISCOUNT GUIDE

Patrick Henry's Catering
624 Kelly Court
Gardnerville, NV 89460
775.781.7154

## LOCAL'S DISCOUNT GUIDE

Full Belly Deli
1267 Hwy 395 Suite B
Gardnerville, NV 89460
775.782.5430

## *The Douglas County Education Foundation thanks you for your support.*

http://www.douglascountyeducationfoundation.org

**2ND CHANCE** FURNITURE CONSIGNMENT

# 10% Off
## Any Item

Expires December 31, 2011

# 2ND CHANCE
## FURNITURE CONSIGNMENT

1492 Hwy 395 N. #104
Gardnerville, NV 89410
775.392.1222

HOURS: Tues-Sat 11-6

Next to Woodette's and
Two Guys from Italy!

## Can't sell your furniture or home furnishings?

# CONSIGN IT!

# Best Kept Secret in the Sierras

## Gardnerville/Minden's
## Best Fashion Boutique
*"A must-stop shopping experience!"*

Attention Brighton-holics!
Visit Northern Nevadas largest
selection of Brighton Jewelry
and accessories at:

# Especially for You
## 1218 Eddy St • Gardnerville
## 775 782 1966

See Carson Map for Directions

*Brighton.*

# 15% Off
## Any Regularly Priced Merchandise
### Excludes Brighton Products
### Not valid with any other promotion
Expires December 31, 2011

ESPECIALLY FOR YOU

106

# Welcome to the Genoa Bar and Saloon,

## Nevada's Oldest Thirst Parlor!

**Plan your next special event:**

Birthday, Anniversary, Wedding, Family Reunion or any other occasion here!!!

Visit our webset for lots of information about us.

www.genoabarandsaloon.com

**GENOA BAR**
NEVADA'S
**OLDEST**
THIRST PARLOR
*Since* 1853

Genoa Bar and Saloon
2282 Main Street
Genoa, NV 89411
775.782.3870

# 20% Off
# Merchandise

**GENOA BAR**
NEVADA'S
**OLDEST**
THIRST PARLOR
*Since* 1853

Expires December 31, 2011

# The Douglas County Education Foundation thanks you for your support.

http://www.douglascountyeducationfoundation.org

*The Douglas County Education Foundation thanks you for your support.*

http://www.douglascountyeducationfoundation.org

*The Douglas County Education Foundation thanks you for your support.*

http://www.douglascountyeducationfoundation.org

**LOCAL'S DISCOUNT GUIDE**

1971 STOR-ALL 2011
www.storall.biz

Stor-All
1456 D. Industrial Way
Gardnerville, NV 89410
775.782.3533

**LOCAL'S DISCOUNT GUIDE**

CANDLES & CRAFTS

Candles N Crafts
1540 Hwy 395, Suite 2
Gardnerville, NV 89410
775.783.3525

## LOCAL'S DISCOUNT GUIDE

# 30% Off
## Total Order

Receive 30% Off Your Entire Purchase

Music Trading Outpost

MUSIC TRADING OUTPOST

Expires December 31, 2011

## LOCAL'S DISCOUNT GUIDE

# 15% Off
## New Merchandise

Come In and Help Us Celebrate Our
19th Anniversary!
Custom Jewelry Design & Manufacturing

Wholesale & Retail

Watch Batteries

Jewelry Appraisals
Insurance Appraisals

HOURS: Mon-Fri 10:30 am-4:30 pm

Van Rensselaer Jewelers

Expires December 31, 2011

## LOCAL'S DISCOUNT GUIDE

MUSIC TRADING OUTPOST

Music Trading Outpost
1302 Langley Dr. Ste 2
Gardnerville, NV 89460
775.265.3200

## LOCAL'S DISCOUNT GUIDE

Van Rensselaer Jewelers

Van Rensselaer Jewelers
1452 Hwy 395
Gardnerville, NV 89410
775.782.3746

**LOCAL'S DISCOUNT GUIDE**

# 20% Off
## Grass Fed Beef

Trimmer Outpost featuring Ranch One all-natural grass fed beef. Visit our Western Gift Shop. Exclusive dealer of Planet X Pottery and Winter Hill Olive Oil made in Nevada specialty products.

Hours:
June-Nov.: Tues-Sun 11-5
December: 7 days a week 10-6
Selling Christmas Trees.
January-May: Weds–Sun 11-5

Expires December 31, 2011

**TRIMMER OUTPOST**
**RANCH ONE**
**ALL-NATURAL BEEF**
Family Ranch • Genoa, Nevada
**(775) 782-2518**

---

**LOCAL'S DISCOUNT GUIDE**

# 20% Off
## Your Entire Purchase

Heartstrings Gallery and Artisan Shop features original watercolors and prints, hand-painted silks, fine art photography, pottery, glass art, jewelry, handmade soaps, and much more...
We also offer art classes!

HOURS: Mon-Sat 10 am-5 pm

**HEARTSTRINGS**
**GALLERY & GIFTS**

Expires December 31, 2011

Local's Discount Guide

Trimmer Outpost

Trimmer Outpost
2276 Main St. P.O. Box 72
Genoa, NV 89411
775.782.2518

Offer validity is governed by the Rules of Use and excludes defined holidays. Offers are not valid with other discount offers unless specified. Coupons void if purchased, sold or bartered. Discounts exclude tax, tip and/or alcohol, where applicable.

Local's Discount Guide

Heartstrings Gallery & Gifts

Heartstrings
1572 Hwy 395
Minden, NV
775.782.0817

Offer validity is governed by the Rules of Use and excludes defined holidays. Offers are not valid with other discount offers unless specified. Coupons void if purchased, sold or bartered. Discounts exclude tax, tip and/or alcohol, where applicable.

**LOCAL'S DISCOUNT GUIDE**

# Angelo's Bootery

4000 Lake Tahoe Blvd
Village Center
Lake Tahoe, CA
530.542.3600

1329 U.S. Hwy 395
Gardnerville, NV
Next to Scolari's
775.782.3322

**LOCAL'S DISCOUNT GUIDE**

# ACE
### The helpful place.

Ace Hardware
1406 Industrial Way
Gardnerville, NV 89410
775.782.5211

121

**LOCAL'S DISCOUNT GUIDE**

**A Wildflower**

Inspiration• Imagination• Creation

A Wildflower Florist
1503 Hwy 395
Gardnerville, NV 89410
775.782.7579

**LOCAL'S DISCOUNT GUIDE**

**SHELBY'S BOOK SHOPPE**

Shelby's Book Shoppe
1663 Lucerne St. Ste C
Minden, NV 89423
775.782.5484

*The Douglas County*
*Education Foundation*
*thanks you for your support.*

http://www.douglascountyeducationfoundation.org

*The Douglas County Education Foundation thanks you for your support.*

http://www.douglascountyeducationfoundation.org

**LOCAL'S DISCOUNT GUIDE**

# Genoa
*Vintage Decor and More*

**Genoa Vintage Decor and More**
P.o. Box 317
2273 S. Main St
Genoa, NV 89411
775.783.1441

**LOCAL'S DISCOUNT GUIDE**

# Aladdin Flowers & Gifts
*Flowers for All Occasions*

**Aladdin Flowers & Gifts**
1411 Hwy 395
Gardnerville, NV 89410
775.782.2655

**COASTAL AIRE** & SHEET METAL

Coastal Aire
2528 Business Pkway #D
Minden, NV 89423

Expires December 31, 2011

# FREE
## Programmable Thermostat
## w/ Purchase

**BBB** MEMBER
Northern Nevada, Inc.

## COASTAL AIRE & SHEET METAL

## ADD ON SPECIALIST

COASTAL AIRE
& SHEET METAL
Heating · Air Conditioning
S-E-A-M-L-E-S-S Rain Gutters
(775) 267-5020

# HEAT & AIR CONDITIONING

### SALES • INSTALLATION
### Service & Repair
### Residential • Commercial
Call Us For All Your Air Conditioning • Heat
Gutter Needs - HVAC/Design & Build

**Aprilaire**
AUTOMATIC HUMIDIFIERS
ELECTRONIC AIR CLEANERS

**22 YEARS OF EXCELLENCE**
Coastal Aire & Sheet Metal

**Rheem**

**bryant**

HOURS: Mon-Fri 7 am-5 pm
Service Calls Available

NV LIC#34523

## FREE ESTIMATES

CA LIC#567013

# 775-882-3377
### CARSON CITY

SENIORS DISCOUNT
MasterCard VISA
SEE OUR COUPON

# 775-267-5020
### MINDEN/GARDNERVILLE

127

# The Douglas County Education Foundation thanks you for your support.

http://www.douglascountyeducationfoundation.org

# The Douglas County Education Foundation thanks you for your support.

http://www.douglascountyeducationfoundation.org

# BOBS PERFORMANCE
## CENTER

Monday - Friday 7:30am-5:30pm * Saturdays 8:00am-1:00pm

### LARGEST RV Supply in Douglas County

---

**Restore Original Mileage & Power Fuel Injection Service**
Machine Flush Fuel Injectors, Clean Throttle Body of deposits & gum build-up, inspect Throttle. (Gas or Diesel)

with coupon, 12/31/2011 **$99.99** plus tax

---

**Oil and Filter Change**
Most Cars and Light Trucks (Gas)

with coupon, 12/31/2011 **$39.95**

Plus Tax & Hazardous Waste
Up to 5 quarts of premium oil

"FREE 25 point inspection"

---

**RV Hot Water Heater Service**
Adjust flame, clean burner tube and heat exchanger & replace Anode Rod

with coupon, 12/31/2011 **$69.95**

---

**Gas and Diesel Brake Service Special**
Replace Front Brakes with Premium Pads, Machine Front Rotors, Lube Calipers, Pins and Slider.

with coupon, expires 12/31/2011 **$189.95** plus tax

---

**Diesel Lube & Oil Change**
Change oil with up to 12 quarts of Delo 15-40W oil, oil filter, all fluids topped off, 25 point inspection & FREE tire rotation.

with coupon, expires 12/31/2011 **$99** Plus Tax & Hazardous Waste

---

**Trailer Wheel Bear Repack**
Clean & inspect brakes, bearings and replace seals. **$99.99**
with coupon,, expires 12/31/2011

**Wheel Alignment with FREE Tire Rotation** **$69.99**
with coupon, 12/31/2011

---

## "From Headlights to Tailpipes"
### 775.782.1958   1417 Industrial Way * Gardnerville

---

## BOBS PERFORMANCE
### CENTER

# Coupon Offers!
# See Above

1417 Industrial Way
Gardnerville, NV 89410
775.782.1958

Expires December 31, 2011

## Affordable Tile & Grout Repair

# *$25.00 Tile Repairs*
## *$1.75/sq. ft. cleaning and sealing.*

Have a brand new shower/tub without the brand new price tag.

Offering installation of ceramic, porcelain, and All Natural Stones.

Affordable Tile & Grout Repair
681 Long Valley
Gardnerville, NV 89460
775.291.0177

Expires December 31, 2011

# *25% Off*
## *Shower Tuneup*
### *Regularly Priced $99*

NO SHOCK ELECTRIC
2572 Heybourne
Minden, NV 89423
775.782.2604 / 775.790.3563

# NO SHOCK
# ELECTRIC

775-782-2604 (msg)
775-790-3563 (cell)

## Remodel ◆ Commercial ◆ Residential
## 20+ Years Experience
## No job too big or small
## 10% Senior Discount

## KEVIN GUNDERSON

# CHRISTENSEN AUTOMOTIVE

# TRAVEL SAFE

## 1539 Hwy 395 N
## Gardnerville, NV 89410
## 775.782.2605

## www.christensenautomotive.com

# $15 Off
# Oil Change

CHRISTENSEN AUTOMOTIVE

Expires December 31, 2011

HOURS: Mon-Fri 7:30 am-5:00 pm

135

# LONE TREE

### FINE ART GALLERY & CUSTOM FRAMING

Celebrating 25 Years Serving Northern Nevada

$25 OFF Custom Framing or Gallery Purchase

Valued at $125 Or More

## "15 Years Voted Carson Valley's Best"

Extensive Selection of Today's Framing Products from All Major Manufacturers

Visit One of the Region's Finest Galleries

*"Where the Spirit of Western Nevada Comes Alive"*

## Lone Tree Gallery
## 1598 Esmeralda
## Minden, NV
## 775-782-2522

# www.lonetreegallery. net

**Baxter Backhoe**

# 1 Hour FREE
### w/3 hour or more job

Expires December 31, 2011

# Baxter Backhoe
-------------------------------------------------

**I would like to introduce myself. My name is Kirk Baxter. I have over 30 years of experience in the construction business.**

- *Septic Systems*
- *Underground Utilities*
- *Irrigation Ditches*
- *House Pads & Footings*
- *Trenching*

## Honest & Reliable • Reasonable

If you have any Excavation needs please call and I will call you back!

# 790-1127

**30 Years Construction Experience • We Handle all Phases of Excavation**

*The Douglas County Education Foundation thanks you for your support.*

http://www.douglascountyeducationfoundation.org

## CARSON CITY
Processing Plant:
Bobby Page's Dry Cleaners
1310 S. Stewart St.
(775) 882-6262
*Same day service offered*

Winnie Center Dry Cleaners
156 W. Winnie Lane
(775) 882-9285

Bobby Page's Dry Cleaners
3173 Hwy 50 East
(775) 884-4844
Open Every Day 7 am-9 pm
Next to Wash Tubs Coin Laundry
Carson's Newest 72 Washer Store

## GARDNERVILLE
Bobby Page's Dry Cleaners
1516 Hwy 395
Haas Center
(775) 782-2911

### Bobby Page's (Roundhill)
Zephyr Cove, NV
Next to Safeway
(775) 588-8066

**Bobby Page's**
DRY CLEANERS
&
Shirt Laundry

## Our #1 Goal is to Earn Your Business

# Melvin's
# CAR WASH & DETAIL

## 1677 HIGHWAY 395 - MINDEN, NV. 89423
## 775-783-4872

## HOURS: Mon-Sat 8:00 am-5:00 pm, Sunday 8:00 am-2:00 pm

*Gift Certificates Available*

*Pre-Paid Booklets Available at Discounted Rates*

*No Appointments Necessary*

**$2 Off** *Any Wash on Sun-Weds*

**$10 Off** *Clay & Wax on Any Day*

**$20 Off** *Full Detail on Mon-Weds*

*Melvin's*

Expires December 31, 2011

Coupon Needed for Discounted Prices

144

## LOCAL'S DISCOUNT GUIDE

BOBULA'S SEPTIC
1950

**Bobula's Septic Service**
**860 Hwy 395 N.**
**Gardnerville, NV 89410**
**775.265.2520**

## *Prompt • Reliable • Competitive*

## LOCAL'S DISCOUNT GUIDE

# Fas-Break®
**Windshield Repair and Replacement Glass Systems**

Fas-Break
1417 Purple Sage Dr.
Gardnerville, NV 89460
775.265.9491

**LOCAL'S DISCOUNT GUIDE**

Steve Figueroa Agency
P.O. Box 2848
Gardnerville, NV 89410
775.782.5339
Email: SJFigins @ gmail.com

**LOCAL'S DISCOUNT GUIDE**

1971 STOR-ALL 2011
www.storall.biz

Stor-All
1456 D. Industrial Way
Gardnerville, NV 89410
775.782.3533

149

**LOCAL'S DISCOUNT GUIDE**

*Van Rensselaer Jewelers*

Van Rensselaer Jewelers
1452 Hwy 395
Gardnerville, NV 89410
775.782.3746

**LOCAL'S DISCOUNT GUIDE**

**GARDNERVILLE AUTOMOTIVE & TRANSMISSION**

Gardnerville Automotive
P.O. Box 367
Gardnerville, NV 89410
775.782.4705

LOCAL'S DISCOUNT GUIDE

# 10% Off
## Event

Private Event Location
Offering the Perfect Country
Setting for Weddings.
Great Spot for Classes,
Sessions, or Special Events
Inside the 150 Year Old Barn or
In the Tranquil Yard.
Please Inquire.

HOURS: Fri-Sun 12-5 pm

Expires December 31, 2011

*Rustic Romance*
**HISTORICAL BARN**
**circa1857**

# The Douglas County Education Foundation thanks you for your support.

http://www.douglascountyeducationfoundation.org

**LOCAL'S DISCOUNT GUIDE**

## Rustic Romance

**HISTORICAL BARN**
circa 1857

Rustic Romance
P.O. Box 317
Genoa, NV 89411
775.783.1441

# The Douglas County Education Foundation thanks you for your support.

http://www.douglascountyeducationfoundation.org

## LOCAL'S DISCOUNT GUIDE

## Mort's Auto Body

Mort's Auto Body, Inc.
1412 Industrial Way
Gardnerville, NV 89410
775.782.8888

## LOCAL'S DISCOUNT GUIDE

Computer Works
Gardnerville, NV 89410
775.720.8348

**LOCAL'S DISCOUNT GUIDE**

Joe's Farrier Service
P.O. Box 682
Minden, NV 89423
775.450.4220

**LOCAL'S DISCOUNT GUIDE**

*Stiehler* GUITARS
Christian Guitar Works Inc.

Christian Guitar Works
775.266.3663
Call for more information

**LOCAL'S DISCOUNT GUIDE**

# Angelo's Bootery

**1329 U.S. Hwy 395
Gardnerville, NV
Next to Scolari's
Garnerville: 775.782.3322
Tahoe: 530.542.3600**

**LOCAL'S DISCOUNT GUIDE**

## Accurate Mobile Locksmith
24 hour locksmith service – Licensed, Bonded & Insured

**Accurate Mobile Locksmith
P.O. Box 840
Minden, NV 89423
775.265.7444
883.8444**

**LOCAL'S DISCOUNT GUIDE**

**≡Helwig Plumbing Co.**
Residential Commercial Service & Repair

**Remodel & New Construction**

**Backflow Certification**
**Don Helwig - Owner**

NV Lic # 74731
**(775) 790-6917**
dhelwig@charter.net
CA Lic # 524692

*SERVING CARSON CITY, MINDEN, GVILLE, AND S. LAKE TAHOE*

# $15 Off
## Service Call
### with this coupon

Expires December 31, 2011

---

**LOCAL'S DISCOUNT GUIDE**

# 10% Off
## All Your Electrical Needs

- Residential-Commercial
- Remodel
- New Construction
- Troubleshooting
- Free Estimates
- Senior Discounts

NV Lic #0073186

**KRUGER**
**Electric Corp.**

Expires December 31, 2011

# SERVICE

## LOCAL'S DISCOUNT GUIDE

### Helwig Plumbing Co.
**Residential Commercial Service & Repair**

Helwig Plumbing Co.
1463 Angora Dr.
Gardnerville, NV 89460
775.790.6917

## LOCAL'S DISCOUNT GUIDE

### KRUGER Electric Corp.

Krugar Electric Corp.
P.O. Box 1563
Gardnerville, NV 89410
775.691.5897

*The Douglas County Education Foundation thanks you for your support.*

http://www.douglascountyeducationfoundation.org

## SERVICE

*The Douglas County Education Foundation thanks you for your support.*

http://www.douglascountyeducationfoundation.org

# "C" and Company
## Salon and Spa

# 10% Off
**One Manicure or Pedicure or One In-Stock Redken Hair Product**

Expires December 31, 2011

1577 3rd Street
Minden, NV 89423
775-783-9883
Call for appointment

**SoLo**
*A Salon*

*Laura*
Stylist, Owner

1679 Hwy. 395, Suite F
Minden, NV 89423
775.783.0707

**Free Haircut** with **Color Service**
**(New Clients Only)**

**Free Manicure** with **Pedicure**

Expires December 31, 2011

# 3 FREE CLASSES at K2 Pilates!
## Your choice:
## PILATES, SPIN or The K2 - or 1 of EACH!

Call to Schedule: 775.783.9033 • www.k2pilates.com • 1512 Hwy 395 - Gardnerville

One coupon per customer.

Expires December 31, 2011

Strength ◊ Balance ◊ Flexibility

## A PILATES and SPIN Studio

◊ Allegro "Tower" Reformers    ◊ Star Trac Pro SPIN Bikes
◊ MVE Pilates Chairs           ◊ Star Track Pro SPIN Computers

### *Improve your health and fitness at K2 Pilates!*

Over 30 classes offered per week, morning and evening class times available

Try the "K2" a 1-hour class featuring 30 minutes of SPIN followed by 30 minutes Pilates

# www.K2pilates.com

1512 Hwy. 395 Suite 4, Gardnerville  -  775.783.9033

## Voted Carson Valley's BEST Pilates Studio!

# *Bohner* CHIROPRACTIC

# Steven L. Bohner, D.C.
## *Wellness care since 1989*

### Chronic Pain & Stress Relief
### Auto - Work - Sports Injuries

### Preferred Provider for
### Most Insurance Companies

## *2 Locations*
## *Minden & Yerington*

1653 Lucerne, Suite C
Minden, NV 89423
(775) 782-5221          Fax (775) 783-8512

25 Littell St.
Yerington, NV 89447
(775) 463-2500

# PAIN?

If you suffer from
• Sciatica • Disc Pain • Neck Pain • Low Back Pain
or pain, numbness, tingling in your buttocks, legs, or arms...

## HAVE YOU BEEN TOLD SURGERY IS YOUR ONLY OPTION?

## FINALLY THE ANSWER!

# Spinal Decompression

This revolutionary

**Non-Surgical Medical Technology**
has helped to effectively treat the cause of
radiating low back leg or arm pain!

---

*Please mention code No. 799*

## Gift Certificate
### Two FREE treatments ($350 value!)
(Must be approved by Doctor T. Vondruska, DC. Limited to qualifying candidates)

**Alpine Spine Center**
**Now serving Carson Valley**
**775.781.0481**

Dr. Tom Vondruska, DC, F.A.S.B.E.
Expiration Date: Dec. 31, 2011

**LOCAL'S DISCOUNT GUIDE**

# 50% Off
## First Session

Are you feeling a little stressed? Find relief at the Sacred Spiral Studio. We have holistic, natural remedies for the body, mind and Spirit! Michele Noel Gabler M.Ms, health practitioner and artist

Sacred Spiral Studio

Call for appointment
775-782-4313

Expires December 31, 2011

---

**LOCAL'S DISCOUNT GUIDE**

# 20% Off
## 1st Treatment

Electrolysis/Laser
Sally Battista - California and Nevada Licensed Permanent Hair Removal.

Complimentary consultations.
Contact Sally at 775-782-6190
1540 Hwy 395, Gardnerville

HOURS: Tues-Sat
By appt, evenings available.

THE SOCIETY FOR CLINICAL & MEDICAL HAIR REMOVAL, INC. • SCMHR •

Expires December 31, 2011

LOCAL'S DISCOUNT GUIDE

Sacred Spiral Studio

Sacred Spiral
1558 First St
Minden, NV 89423
775.782.4313

Offer validity is governed by the Rules of Use and excludes defined holidays. Offers are not valid with other discount offers unless specified. Coupons void if purchased, sold or bartered. Discounts exclude tax, tip and/or alcohol, where applicable.

LOCAL'S DISCOUNT GUIDE

THE SOCIETY FOR CLINICAL & MEDICAL HAIR REMOVAL, INC. • SCMHR •

Electrolysis Clinic
Sally Battista, RE, CME
1540 Hwy 395
Gardnerville, NV 89410
775.782.6190

Offer validity is governed by the Rules of Use and excludes defined holidays. Offers are not valid with other discount offers unless specified. Coupons void if purchased, sold or bartered. Discounts exclude tax, tip and/or alcohol, where applicable.

**LOCAL'S DISCOUNT GUIDE**

**body**language
health and wellbeing

Body Language
1478 B 4th Street
Minden, NV 89423
775.782.8485

**LOCAL'S DISCOUNT GUIDE**

**PEAK NUTRITION**
DISCOUNT SPORTS NUTRITION

Peak Nutrition
1547 US Hwy 395 N.
Minden, NV 89423
775.782.2244

**LOCAL'S DISCOUNT GUIDE**

Shear Heaven Salon Da Spa
1328 Highway 395 Suite 301
Gardnerville, NV 89410
775.782.3115

**LOCAL'S DISCOUNT GUIDE**

Fifth Street
Salon

Fifth Street Salon
1604 Esmeralda Ave #202
Minden, NV 89423
775.782.2813

**LOCAL'S DISCOUNT GUIDE**

## FREE
### Eyebrow Wax
*One per coupon*

Organic Skin Care Products
Facials
Full Service Waxing
Glominerals Makeup
with Licensed Esthetician
Brooke Roberts
Since 2002

HOURS: Tues-Sat appt. only

*Serendipity Skin Care*

Expires December 31, 2011

---

**LOCAL'S DISCOUNT GUIDE**

## 2 For 1 Single Tan
## 20% Off Apparel
### $20 Mystic Tan (reg. $30)

Tahoe & Minden's Only Upscale
Tanning & Apparel Store

"Come as a Customer
Leave as a Friend"

Minden & Tahoe's Only Location

HOURS: Open 7 Days a Week

Expires December 31, 2011

**LOCAL'S DISCOUNT GUIDE**

*Serendipity Skin Care*

Serendipity Skin Care
1255 Hwy 395 Suite B
Gardnerville, NV 89410
775.790.3797

**LOCAL'S DISCOUNT GUIDE**

Sunsational Tans
1659 Hwy 395 #B
Minden, NV
775.782.2552

**LOCAL'S DISCOUNT GUIDE**

Tru Hair Studio
244 Dayton Valley Rd
Suite 104
Dayton, NV 89403
775.246.4445

**LOCAL'S DISCOUNT GUIDE**

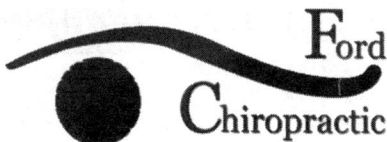

Ford Chiropractic

Ford Chiropractic
1701 County Road Ste L
Minden, NV 89423
775.782.1000

*The Douglas County Education Foundation thanks you for your support.*

http://www.douglascountyeducationfoundation.org

*The Douglas County Education Foundation thanks you for your support.*

http://www.douglascountyeducationfoundation.org

**Purple Sage**
Equine Services

Offering training lessons colt starting and clinics for all disciplines utilizing methods made popular by Dorrance/Hunt/Brannaman. Come learn The Three R's of Horsemanship.

Expires December 31, 2011

# 50% Off
## First Lesson

Purple Sage
Equine Services

The "3 R's" of Horsemanship

Relaxed — Responsive — Respectful

Clinics - Lessons - Training - Colt Starting
Ranch - Show - Trail - English & Western - All Breeds
775-901-6999 Karyn Shirley www.purplesageequine.com

# Guns N Arrows
## 1507 Hwy 395, Gardnerville
## 775-783-1858

## Rifles, Handguns, Shotguns, Ammunition & Accessories
## In House AR-15 Armorer
## Custom Firearm Duracoat Service
### Gunsmithing

# Buy - Sell - Trade
## Firearms Estate Liquidation
## Consignment Specialists

# OPEN MONDAY TO SATURDAY 9AM-5PM
## www.gunsnarrows.com

**Coupon**

Guns N Arrows

**15% Discount on all accessories with Firearm Purchase**

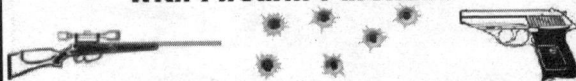

Discount must be take at time of purchase of Firearm

Expires December 31, 2011

182

# Free Medium Popcorn*
## *with the purchase of a Medium Drink

Come visit us on the web at **www.ironwoodcinemas8.com**

Expires December 31, 2011

# TOSS ONCE, TOSS TWICE AND YOU'RE HOOKED

THIS CORN BAG TOSS GAME HAS COME TO THE WEST! THE GAME THAT'S SEEN AT FOOTBALL TAILGATE PARTIES, NASCAR EVENTS, RENO ACES BALLGAMES AND THOUSANDS OF BACKYARD BBQ'S IS HERE, AND WE'RE PROUD TO MAKE YOU THE BEST QUALITY REGULATION BOARDS IN THE WEST, IF NOT THE NATION. THIS GAME IS ENJOYED BY ALL AGES & GENDERS. PLAYED LIKE HORSESHOES BUT WITHOUT THE DOWNSIDES OF FLYING STEEL, MAKING OF PITS AND AGE LIMITS. OUR BOARDS ARE PORTABLE SO YOU CAN TAKE 'EM ANYWHERE. DUE TO OUR EAGERNESS TO INTRODUCE THIS FUN AND EXCITING GAME TO THE AREA, WE ARE OFFERING A 20% DISCOUNT ON ALL OF OUR BOARD SETS (SETS INCLUDE TWO BOARDS AND EIGHT BAGS).
VISIT OUR WEBSITE: WWW.HIGHCOUNTRYCORNHOLE.COM
TO LEARN MORE OR CALL 775-265-2522

# RAVEN GAMZ

# 20% Off
## All Our Board Sets

Expires December 31, 2011

## Want to start your own league?
## Call Tim or Greg for details!
## 265-5454

# BOWLING
# SPECIALS

### Mondays*
$2 per game Bowling

### Wednesdays**
$5 All-you-can-Bowl

*Shoe Rental extra.
**2 Hour Limit. Shoe Rental extra.

**SILVER STRIKE**

## Tillman Center • Gardnerville Ranchos
## 1281 Kimmerling Road • 775-265-5454

# *FREE Shoe Rental*
## *Max 4 Persons per Coupon*
### *w/ minimum 2 games each*

Expires December 31, 2011

Want to start your own league?
Call Tim or Greg for details!
265-5454

BOWLING
SPECIALS
Mondays*
$2 per game Bowling
Wednesdays**
$5 All-you-can-Bowl

*Shoe Rental extra.
**2 Hour Limit. Shoe Rental extra.

SILVER STRIKE

# 10% Off
## Your Special Event
## or the Harvest Festival

**HISTORIC WESTERN WORKING RANCH**

Expires December 31, 2011

# THE CORLEY RANCH

## HISTORIC WESTERN WORKING RANCH & EVENTS AREA

895 Hwy 395, Gardnerville, Nevada 89410

775-721-1047

www.corleyranch.com

# The Douglas County Education Foundation thanks you for your support.

http://www.douglascountyeducationfoundation.org

# The Douglas County Education Foundation thanks you for your support.

http://www.douglascountyeducationfoundation.org

**LOCAL'S DISCOUNT GUIDE**

**WOW WAKEPLACE .COM**
**Western Oasis Wakeplace**

Wow
2900 Hwy 395
Minden, NV 89423
775.267.9738

**LOCAL'S DISCOUNT GUIDE**

**Carson Valley**
**GOLF COURSE**

Carson Valley Golf Course
1027 Riverview Drive
Gardnerville, NV
Tee Times 775.265.3181
carsonvalleygolf.com

**GENOA COUNTRY INN**

## 10% Off
### room rates

**GENOA COUNTRY INN**

2292 Main Street P.O. Box 713 Genoa, Nevada 89411

# 775-782-4500

We Offer
Luxury Rooms, In Room Coffee, Microwaves,
Refrigerators, 32" Flat Screen Televisions, Wireless
Internet and Balconies with a View. The staff is friendly,
knowledgeable and will make you feel right at home.

Website: GenoaCountryInn.com
E-mail: GenoaCountryInn@gmail.com

**Best Western**

# MINDEN INN

1795 Ironwood Drive
Minden, NV 89423

(775) 782-7766            Toll Free # (866) 441-1234

## Stay Two Nights
## Third Night FREE

**Best Western**

Offer excludes weekends in months July and August

Expires December 31, 2011

# The Douglas County Education Foundation thanks you for your support.

http://www.douglascountyeducationfoundation.org

# Lake Tahoe/ Truckee

# Fine Dining | Bar & Lounge | Events

N

Zephyr Cove

50

Zephyr Heights Village

Marla Bay

Lake Tahoe

Nevada
California

Kingsbury Grade

50

207

Stateline

BISTRO
DANIELLE

Real. Local. Cuisine.

775.586.1070 | 605 Hwy. 50 | Zephyr Heights, NV 89448
Open 5pm to 10pm | Tuesday through Saturday
Fine Dining | Bar & Lounge | Events

Located on Highway 50 in Zephyr Heights, NV.
Two miles North of Stateline and one mile
South of Zephyr Cove, across from Marla Bay.

# 775.586.1070 | www.BistroDanielle.com

## Lake Tahoe Cruises
## Zephyr Cove Resort

# The Dining Room is adorned with a Large Stone Fireplace and has a View of Lake Tahoe.

*Come Try Our Healthy Portions Near the Shore of Lake Tahoe in Historic Zephyr Cove.*

## Buy One Entree Get the Second Entree Free
*Pay for entree of greater value.*

Expires December 31, 2011

**Lake Tahoe Cruises Zephyr Cove Resort**

## Bella Vita Catering
### "The Good Life"

Distinctive catering for all occasions, From an intimate evening for 2 to a festive party for 500.

Bella Vita specializes in all the little details that will make your event truly successful.

**Hot & cold Appetizers** (Bruschetta, Assorted Crostini, Pesto Torta, Prawn Butter served with Baguettes)

**Soup & Salads** (Greek, Caesar, Potato, Pasta, etc)

**Sandwiches** (Meatloaf; Chicken, Egg and Tuna Salad; Turkey, etc)

**Entrees** (Seafood Paella, Fettucini Alfredo, Tri Tip served w/Tri Sauces, Chicken Chardonnay, etc)

**Sushi** (Classic raw, cooked classic rolls, customer rolls, etc)

**Desserts** (Mini Cream Puffs, Brownies, Cheesecakes, Mousse, etc)

This is just a sampling of some of the delicious menu items we offer, we are always happy to work with you on custom menus!

**775-783-9475 phone / 775-783-9476 fax**

# www.bellavitacateringtgl.com

# Buy 1 Entrée
# Get 2nd Free
### *Of equal or lesser value. Present Coupon.*

**Austin's**
Mountain Country Food
& Spirits

Expires December 31, 2011          120 Country Club  Incline Village, NV 89450   775.832.7778

**Austin's**
**Mountain Country Food**
**& Spirits**

## *Located Across from the Hyatt in Incline Village.*

We serve homestyle American cusine made fresh from scratch daily. Super salad bowls, rib eye steaks, chicken fried chicken, fresh fish, vegetarian options, your choice of side dishes, home made pies, kids menu and a full bar.

## 120 Country Club
## Incline Village, NV 89450
## 775.832.7778

## Located at the West End of Commercial Row
## Historic Downtown Truckee
## HOURS: Daily 11 am-9 pm

204

# 10% Off
## Food Only

## Hacienda de la Sierra
*at incline village*

### Voted "Best Mexican Restaurant" Year After Year!
– *North Tahoe Truckee Review* Readers' Survey

### Open Daily From 4pm
Serving Lunch Christmas Week 12/26 thru 1/1

### Happy Hour
Mon.-Fri. 4-6pm

www.haciendatahoe.com
**Located at 931 Tahoe Blvd., Incline Village**
Across the street from Raley's • (775)831-8300

### Serving Lunch Memorial Day Through Labor Day and Christmas Week

# Thank you for your continued support of the Tahoe Truckee Unified School District.

www.ttusd.com

*River Grill*
tahoe city, ca

*River Grill*
tahoe city, ca

*River Grill*
tahoe city, ca

# 2 For 1
## 2 Course Minimum
## of Equal or Lesser Value

Expires December 31, 2011

*River Grill*
tahoe city, ca

2 Course Minimum. Not valid with any other discount. Not valid for parties of 10 or more. Not valid 12/16 to 1/18 and 2/11/2011 to 2/28/2011, 5/26/2011 to 9/30/2011. Free entree is of equal or lesser value.

# Free Latte or Junior Cone
### with purchase of equal or greater value

## 530 600-0690
3660 Lake Tahoe Blvd
South Lake Tahoe, CA

# The Red Hut Cafe

2749 Lake Tahoe Boulevard, South Lake Tahoe, California 96150 USA
Telephone: 530-541-9024
227 Kingsbury Grade, Stateline @ Lake Tahoe, Nevada 89449 USA
Telephone: 775-588-7488
Ski Run Center, 3660 Lake Tahoe Blvd, South Lake Tahoe, California 96150
Telephone: 530-544-1595

**www.redhutcafe.com**

# Thank you for your continued support of the Tahoe Truckee Unified School District.

www.ttusd.com

**Local's Discount Guide**

# FREE
## Beer or Soda
### w/Eat-In Pizza Order

Your Local Pizza Since 1988

In the Village Center across from the Post Office

Eat In & Take Out • Baked or U-Bake • Full Bar • Gaming

**BAR BAR BAR**

**Pizza**

Expires December 31, 2011

---

**Local's Discount Guide**

# 1/2 Off
## 2nd Entree*

*with purchase of 1st entree & beverage of equal or lesser value

Crosby's Pub & Casino
868 Tahoe Blvd Ste #4
Incline Village, NV 89450
HOURS: 9 am-10 pm

**Crosby's**
We Serve Fun!

GRILL
PUB
CASINO

Expires December 31, 2011

Bar Bar Bar Pizza
760 Mays Blvd
Incline Village, NV 89451
775.831.2700

Crosby's Pub & Casino
868 Tahoe Blvd Ste #4
Incline Village, NV 89450

**LOCAL'S DISCOUNT GUIDE**

# Take $2 Off
## A Char-Pit Combo Meal

Char-Pits
Family Rib Special

Family Rib, Full French Fries,
Full Onion Rings, Full Chipotle
Coleslaw and Five Chicken Strips

All for $26.99
Half Rib Special
Half Rib, French Fries, Chipotle,
Coleslaw, and Two Chicken Strips
$10.99
Please Call for Carry Out!!!

"World Famous Char-Broiler Since 1962"

1/4 LB.

## CHAR-PIT
BURGERS - RIBS - CHICKEN
FISH & CHIPS - FROSTIES

Expires December 31, 2011

---

**LOCAL'S DISCOUNT GUIDE**

# Buy One Get One 1/2 Off
### (equal or lesser value)
**(Bowl of Soup, Full Salad, Or Full Sandwich)**

4 Seasons Soup & Salad Cafe
3434 Lake Tahoe Blvd
So Lake Tahoe, CA 96150
530.541.4787

HOURS:
Mon-Sat 11 am-5 pm,
Sun 11 am-4 pm

# 4 Seasons
## Soup & Salad Cafe

Expires December 31, 2011

**LOCAL'S DISCOUNT GUIDE**

*"World Famous Char-Broiler Since 1962"*

1/4 LB.

**CHAR-PIT**

BURGERS - RIBS - CHICKEN
FISH & CHIPS - FROSTIES

Char-Pit, Inc.
P.O. Box 86
Kings Beach, CA 96143
530.546.3171

**LOCAL'S DISCOUNT GUIDE**

4 Seasons Soup & Salad Cafe
3434 Lake Tahoe Blvd
So Lake Tahoe, CA 96150
530.541.4787

## LOCAL'S DISCOUNT GUIDE

# 2 For 1
## Ice Cream Cone

Old fashioned ice cream parlor. Sundaes, Smoothies, Frozen Yogurt, Floats, Espresso Shake

We are located in downtown Truckee.

HOURS: Mon-Sun 11 am-7 pm

# BUD'S ICE CREAM

Expires December 31, 2011

# Thank you for your continued support of the Tahoe Truckee Unified School District.

## www.ttusd.com

LOCAL'S
DISCOUNT
GUIDE

BUD'S
ICE CREAM

Bud's Ice Cream
10108 Donner Pass Rd
Truckee, CA 96161
530.587.3177

# Thank you for your continued support of the Tahoe Truckee Unified School District.

## www.ttusd.com

**LOCAL'S DISCOUNT GUIDE**

# Fox & Hound

LAKE TAHOE BAR & GRILL | ELEVATION 7380

Fox & Hound
237 Tramway Road,
Stateline, NV
775.588.8887

**LOCAL'S DISCOUNT GUIDE**

# MOTT CANYON

tavern&grill•lake tahoe,nv

Mott Canyon Tavern & Grill
259 Kingsbury Grade
Stateline, NV 89449
775.586.1145

**LOCAL'S DISCOUNT GUIDE**

# 2 For 1
## Coffee

Old fashioned home-cooked food.
We are located in downtown
Truckee.

HOURS: Mon-Thurs 6 am-3 pm,
Fri-Sun 6 am-4 pm

Expires December 31, 2011

---

**LOCAL'S DISCOUNT GUIDE**

## ALOHA MONEY

### Aloha ICE CREAM

## 10% OFF purchases

**541-3956**
THE RISE FAMILY
3330 Lake Tahoe Blvd., S.Lake Tahoe,CA 96150

Ice Cream • Baked Goods • Custom Ice Cream Cakes

Expires December 31, 2011

## Local's Discount Guide

**Coffee And**
10106 Donner Pass Rd
Truckee, CA 96161
530.587.3123

## Local's Discount Guide

**Aloha Ice Cream**
P.O. Box 8879
So. Lake Tahoe, CA 96158
530.541.3956

**fat CITY**

**F O O D C O M P A N Y**

Fat City Food Co
2660 LTB
So Lake Tahoe
530.542.2780

Thai One On
292 Kingsbury Ln
Stateline, CA 89449
775.586.8424

We invite you to become a...
Partner in Education.

To become a partner or learn more about the program, contact Coleen DeLong, Partnership Coordinator, Education Alliance at 353-5533 or cdelon@washoe.k12.nv.us.
You will be partnered with a school in our district based on the needs of the school and the resources, desire and capacity of your business or service organization. We will arrange and attend a meeting with you and the school principal to get things started. Partnerships can be started at any time.

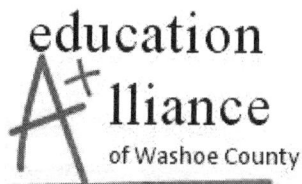

education
A⁺lliance
of Washoe County

* Support Academic Achievement in WCSD
* Provide resources and mentoring to schools and students
*Allow opportunities for your employees to be involved
* Make a positive impact on your community

# Thank you for your continued support of the Tahoe Truckee Unified School District.

www.ttusd.com

**LOCAL'S DISCOUNT GUIDE**

Rocky Mountain
Chocolate Factory
1001 Heavenly Village
South Lake Tahoe, CA 96150
530.600.0235

**LOCAL'S DISCOUNT GUIDE**

Papa Dave's Preowned Furniture
2358 Lake Tahoe Blvd.
So. Lake Tahoe, CA
530.542.1396

**LOCAL'S DISCOUNT GUIDE**

*COMPUTER SALES - SERVICE - REPAIR*

# Floppys

Floppys Computer Stores stock a complete
selection of new and used desktop computers,
laptops, netbooks, printers, ink and toner,
networking, routers, memory upgrades
and lots of other computer parts.
## ALL AT GUARANTEED LOWEST PRICES

**LOCAL'S DISCOUNT GUIDE**

Grass Roots Natural Foods
2040 Dunlap Dr.
So. Lake Tahoe 96150
530.541.7788

# Grass Roots
**NATURAL FOODS**

**LOCAL'S DISCOUNT GUIDE**

# 10% Off
## Any Purchase

10-15% Off Selected Fireplaces

HOURS:
Mon-Fri 9 am-5 pm,
Sat 10 am-2 pm

SOUTH Y FIREPLACE

Expires December 31, 2011

---

**LOCAL'S DISCOUNT GUIDE**

# 25% Off
## Entire Purchase
### Buy Item, Get 2nd of Equal or Lesser Value Half Off

Closet Cowgirl
Surf & Turf
Apparel & Accessories

11401 Donner Pass Rd #A
Truckee, CA 96161
530.582.7424

HOURS: Mon-Sat

Closet Cowgirl

Expires December 31, 2011

**Local's Discount Guide**

South Y Fireplace
1961 Lake Tahoe
So Lake Tahoe, CA 96150
530.541.6833

**Local's Discount Guide**

*Closet Cowgirl*

Closet Cowgirl
11401 Donner Pass Rd #A
Truckee, CA 96161
530.582.7424

**LOCAL'S DISCOUNT GUIDE**

# 20% Off
## Retail Only

Decorated Cakes for All Occasions
Delicious Doughnuts, Pies
Cookies & Pastry Specialties
Sandwiches & Ice Cream
Photo-Image Cakes

HOURS: 7 Days a Week 5 am-7 pm

**The Treat Box Bakery**

Expires December 31, 2011

---

**LOCAL'S DISCOUNT GUIDE**

# 20% Off Apparel
## $20 Mystic Tan
### (Reg. $30)

Tahoe & Minden's Best
Tanning & Clothing Store

"Come as a Customer,
Leave as a Friend"

Minden & Tahoe's
Only Location for Mystic Tan

HOURS: Mon-Fri 9 am-9 pm,
Sat 9 am-7 pm, Sun 10 am-6 pm

Expires December 31, 2011

**LOCAL'S DISCOUNT GUIDE**

**The Treat Box Bakery**

The Treat Box Bakery
11400 Donner Pass Rd
Truckee, CA 96161
530.582.6554

**LOCAL'S DISCOUNT GUIDE**

Sunsational Tanning
2227 Lake Tahoe Blvd
So. Lake Tahoe
530.542.8757

**LOCAL'S DISCOUNT GUIDE**

**AutoGlass EXPRESS TRUCKEE**

Autoglass Express Truckee
10825 Pioneer Trail #10613
Truckee, CA 96161
530.550.1314

**LOCAL'S DISCOUNT GUIDE**

**THE POTLATCH**

The Potlatch
930 Tahoe Blvd. Suite 401
Incline Village, NV 89451
775.833.2485

# THE SKY'S THE LIMIT
## Home Cleaning & Property Care
### Since 1998

One Call Does It All!
• Property Management
• Private and Rental Home Cleaning
• Home Repairs • Snow Removal • Yard Cleanup
*Licensed, Bonded, and Insured*

Cell: (530) 546-7800
E-mail: theskysthelimit@onemain.com
PO Box 810
Tahoe City, CA 96145

7495 N. Lake Blvd., Tahoe Vista CA

*Serving All of north shore and west shores from Incline Village to Rubicon , as well as Alpine Meadows, Squaw Valley and Truckee*

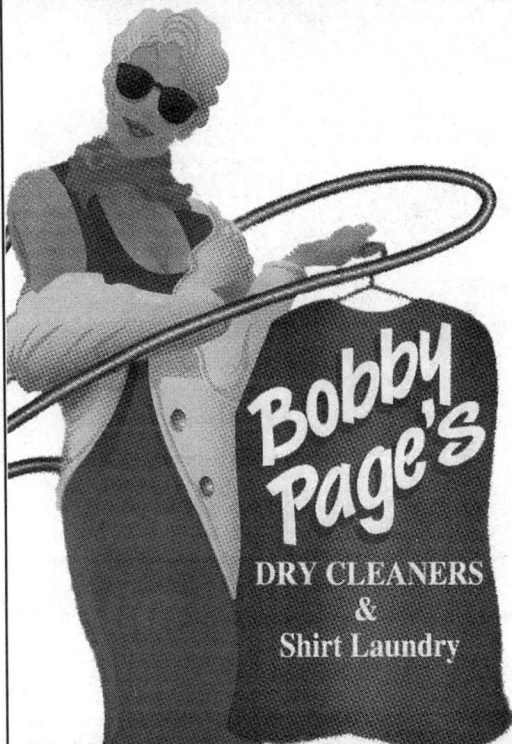

## CARSON CITY
Processing Plant:
Bobby Page's Dry Cleaners
1310 S. Stewart St.
(775) 882-6262
*Same day service offered*

Winnie Center Dry Cleaners
156 W. Winnie Lane
(775) 882-9285

Bobby Page's Dry Cleaners
3173 Hwy 50 East
(775) 884-4844
Open Every Day 7 am-9 pm
Next to Wash Tubs Coin Laundry
Carson's Newest 72 Washer Store

## GARDNERVILLE
Bobby Page's Dry Cleaners
1516 Hwy 395
Haas Center
(775) 782-2911

### Bobby Page's (Roundhill)
Zephyr Cove, NV
Next to Safeway
(775) 588-8066

**Bobby Page's**
DRY CLEANERS
&
Shirt Laundry

## Our #1 Goal is to Earn Your Business

242

**LOCAL'S DISCOUNT GUIDE**

# THE SKY'S THE LIMIT
Home Cleaning & Property Care
Since 1998

The Sky's the Limit
P.O. Box 810
Tahoe City, CA 96145
530.546.7800

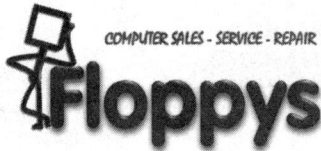

**LOCAL'S DISCOUNT GUIDE**

COMPUTER SALES - SERVICE - REPAIR

**Floppys**

Floppys Computer Stores stock a complete
selection of new and used desktop computers,
laptops, netbooks, printers, ink and toner,
networking, routers, memory upgrades
and lots of other computer parts.
ALL AT GUARANTEED LOWEST PRICES

## LOCAL'S DISCOUNT GUIDE

Road Rash
2218 Lake Tahoe Blvd
South Lake Tahoe, CA 96150
530.541.2518

## LOCAL'S DISCOUNT GUIDE

## Accurate Mobile Locksmith
24 hour locksmith service -- Licensed, Bonded & Insured

**Accurate Mobile Locksmith**
P.O. Box 840
Minden, NV 89423
775.265.7444
883.8444

## LOCAL'S DISCOUNT GUIDE

South Y Fireplace
1961 Lake Tahoe
So Lake Tahoe, CA 96150
530.541.6833

## LOCAL'S DISCOUNT GUIDE

**AutoGlass EXPRESS TRUCKEE**

Autoglass Express Truckee
10825 Pioneer Trail #10613
Truckee, CA 96161
530.550.1314

Thank you for your
continued support of the
Tahoe Truckee Unified
School District.

www.ttusd.com

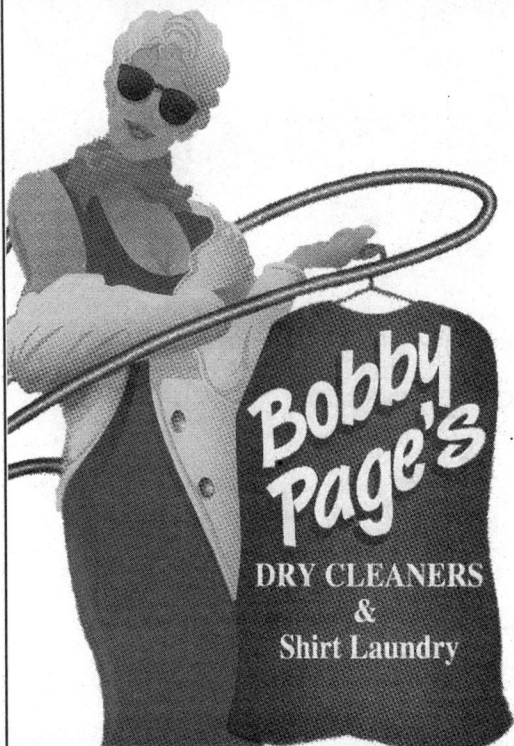

## CARSON CITY

Processing Plant:
Bobby Page's Dry Cleaners
1310 S. Stewart St.
(775) 882-6262
*Same day service offered*

Winnie Center Dry Cleaners
156 W. Winnie Lane
(775) 882-9285

Bobby Page's Dry Cleaners
3173 Hwy 50 East
(775) 884-4844
Open Every Day 7 am-9 pm
Next to Wash Tubs Coin Laundry
Carson's Newest 72 Washer Store

## GARDNERVILLE

Bobby Page's Dry Cleaners
1516 Hwy 395
Haas Center
(775) 782-2911

### Bobby Page's (Roundhill)

Zephyr Cove, NV
Next to Safeway
(775) 588-8066

*Bobby Page's*

DRY CLEANERS
&
Shirt Laundry

## Our #1 Goal is to Earn Your Business

# ALPINE EYECARE
## OPTOMETRY

# New Multi-Focal Contact Lenses

- **Allows you to see distance, near and intermediate vision**
- **No need for bifocals or reading glasses**
- **Extremely comfortable**

*(Not available in astigmatism or color contacts)*

**Mark Michitsch, OD**

# (775) 588-3500
276 Kingsbury Grade, Suite 103
Stateline, Nevada

**Steven L. Kline, OD**

# BALANCE
## *body studios*

- Spin
- Yoga
- Pilates
- Kickboxing
- Massage
- Body Work
- ArtForm®
- Strip 2 Fit
- Dance Classes
- Personal Training
- *And much more!*

**balancebodystudios.com**
775.580.7267 | 276 Kingsbury Grade
Next to 7Eleven | Walk-Ins Welcome

**$2 off**
Your First Drop-In Class
BALANCE

Expires December 31, 2011

# BALANCE
## *body studios*
**balancebodystudios.com**

**ANYTIME FITNESS.**

# 1st 2 Mos. Free
## No Enrollment or Processing Fee

*Restrictions: Must agree to a 12 mo. contract*
*Zephyr Cove location only*

Expires December 31, 2011

# ANYTIME FITNESS.

## *OPEN 24 HOURS* for Members and Walk-ins Welcome

## 212 Elks Point Road #550
## Zephyr Cove, NV 89448
## (775) 580-7266
## www.anytimefitness.com

Text VIPTEXTCLUB ANYTIMEFITNESS to 368638
to receive special offers.

# Relax with Rita
# Massage Therapy

- Unwind, Enjoy, Refresh
- Spa Therapy/Reflexology
- Sports and Medical Massage
- Mobile Services Available to the North Lake/Truckee Area
- Specializing in all disciplines of massage

P.O. Box 8013
Truckee, CA 96162
530.513.7632

## $20 Off

*Your First Hour Appointment*
*(not available with other promotions)*

Expires December 31, 2011

# Relax
# with Rita

Thank you for your continued support of the Tahoe Truckee Unified School District.

www.ttusd.com

**LOCAL'S DISCOUNT GUIDE**

Shag Hair Studio

Shag Hair Studio
11401 Donner Pass Rd #A
Truckee, CA 96161
Call Celeste at 530.414.0617

# Thank you for your continued support of the Tahoe Truckee Unified School District.

www.ttusd.com

257

**BLEU WAVE CRUISES**

## RESORT DISCOUNTS

### $10.00 OFF
Per Person

**Emerald Bay LUNCH CRUISE**

### $5.00 OFF
Per Person

**Emerald Bay SIGHTSEEING CRUISE**

For Reservations    775-588-WAVE (9283)

## See Above For Special Offers!

**BLEU WAVE CRUISES**

Expires December 31, 2011

259

# 2 FOR 1 BEGINNER PACKAGE

Enjoy one complimentary first time beginner ski or snowboard package
when a second first time beginner ski or snowboard package of equal
or greater value is purchased. Not valid Dec. 20, 2010 – Jan. 2, 2011
and Feb 16, 2011-Feb 26, 2011. Not Valid for Child Ski Center.
Offer expires at end of 2010-2011 winter season.

1210 Ski Way, Incline Village, NV 89451 • 775.832.1177
www.DiamondPeak.com

**Diamond Peak**
INCLINE VILLAGE LAKE TAHOE

Present this coupon at resort
for discount.

# THE PERFECT PASS FOR BEGINNERS
## After Your First Lesson Check Out Our Beginner Pass.

$\$109$

Valid everyday of the season.
For Schoolhouse and Lodgepole lifts only.
Can be upgraded at anytime to full access pass.

**(775) 832-1177**
For more information visit:
www.diamondpeak.com

**Diamond Peak**
INCLINE VILLAGE LAKE TAHOE

Your Tahoe Place.

# Bowl Incline
## North Shore's Complete Family Recreation Center
### VOTED BEST POOL ROOM ON THE NORTH SHORE!

- Automatic Scoring
- "Bumper Bowling"
- Video Arcade
- Billiards
- Video Poker
- Cocktails
- ATM
- Full Swing Golf Simulator
- Air Conditioned!
- Smoke Free Every Day!

920 Southwood Blvd., Incline Village
(775) 831-1900
email: bowlink@aol.com

## FREE BOWLING
**Each person who bowls 2 games at regular price gets a 3rd game free with this coupon.**

## Bowl Incline

Expires December 31, 2011

Coupon Good for the entire party. Limit 1 free game per person per visit. Not valid with other offers. Not valid for league or tournament play.

**Lake Tahoe Cruises**
**Zephyr Cove Resort**

# Buy One Adult Ticket
# Get the Second
# Ticket Free
### For Same Day Cruises on
### the M.S. Dixie or Tahoe Queen

Expires December 31, 2011

# Lake Tahoe Cruises
# Zephyr Cove Resort

## There is No Better Way to
## Take in the Beauty of Emerald Bay
## than on the Water itself, so
## Come Aboard the Tahoe Queen
## or M.S. Dixie and Enjoy a Real
## Tahoe Must-Do
## *www.zephyrcove.com for times*

# Thank you for your continued support of the Tahoe Truckee Unified School District.

www.ttusd.com

**LOCAL'S DISCOUNT GUIDE**

# Free
## 1/2 Hour Pool

Classic Cue
530-541-8704

Hours:
Sun-Sat 11:30 am-12 am
Based on availability
Limit 1 coupon per visit

**Classic Cue**

Expires December 31, 2011

---

**LOCAL'S DISCOUNT GUIDE**

# 2 For 1
## Sledding

**G Granlibakken**
CONFERENCE CENTER & LODGE • LAKE TAHOE

Two for one sledding - includes saucer and use of the
hill. ALL DAY. Historic Skiing & Sledding Hill.

Ski Season Dec to April

Expires December 31, 2011

**LOCAL'S DISCOUNT GUIDE**

*Classic Cue*

Classic Cue
1961 B Lake Tahoe Blvd.
South Lake Tahoe, CA 96150
530.541.8704

**LOCAL'S DISCOUNT GUIDE**

**G Granlibakken**
CONFERENCE CENTER & LODGE · LAKE TAHOE

Granlibakken Resort
725 Granlibakken
Tahoe City, CA 96145
530.583.4242

**LOCAL'S DISCOUNT GUIDE**

Adrift Tahoe
8338 North Lake Blvd
Kings Beach, CA 96143
888.676.7702

**LOCAL'S DISCOUNT GUIDE**

**TAHOE BIKE & SKI**

Tahoe Bike & Ski
8499 N. Lake Blvd
Kings Beach
530.546.7437

# Inn at Truckee

# *Stay Two Nights Get 3rd Night Free*

**Offer not valid weekends and holidays.**

The Inn at Truckee

11506 Deerfield Drive  Truckee, CA
530.587.8888 ✖ 888.773.6888
www.innattruckee.com

# TRUCKEE DONNER

## L O D G E

The Truckee Donner Lodge is nestled in the heart of the Sierra Nevada mountains only minutes from Lake Tahoe and Donner Lake. The lodge is uniquely designed with relaxation and convenience in mind. Rooms are well appointed and breakfast is included. The lodge, seconds from historic downtown Truckee, is on the doorstep of wonderful restaurants, shops, nightlife and an unrivaled recreational paradise, surrounded by lakes and magnificent mountains.

**10527 COLDSTREAM RD., TRUCKEE, CA 96161**
**877.878.2533 | 530.582.9999**
**WWW.TRUCKEEDONNERLODGE.COM**

*AAA* ◆◆◆

## Stay Two Nights
## Get 3rd Night Free
*Offer not valid weekends and holidays.*

**Truckee
Donner Lodge**

Expires December 31, 2011

# NOTES

# NOTES

# NOTES

# NOTES

# NOTES

# NOTES

# Reno/Sparks

# Buy Any Entree and 2 Drinks
# Get 2nd Entree* FREE
## *2nd Entree of Equal or Lesser Value
**Dine in Only. All Locations. Not Valid with any other offer.**
**One Coupon per table.**

Expires December 31, 2011

# BEST GRUB & GROG IN TOWN!

**Breakfast**
Sat & Sun Only
9 am-12 noon

**Lunch & Dinner**
Open 7 Days a Week

FLOWING TIDE
PUB

| 4690 Longley @ Mira Loma | 465 S. Meadows Pkwy #5 | 10580 N. McCarran |
|---|---|---|
| (Former Spiro's Location) | Next to Wells Fargo | Save Mart Shopping Ctr. |
| **284-7610** | **284-7707** | **747-7707** |

279

# BRAIDO's
## DELI-CAFE

775-827-2777
6147 Lakeside Drive suite 102
Reno, NV 89511
www.braidosdelicafe.com

## Buy One, Get One
# Half Off

### BRAIDO's
#### DELI-CAFE

Expires December 31, 2011

281

# MR. PICKLE'S SANDWICH SHOP

*Deli and Catering Service in Sparks, Nevada*

*Under New Ownership*

**Serving the finest Gourmet Sandwiches, Hot Dogs, Soups and Salads.**

**We have only the Freshest Varieties of Breads and Rolls from The Truckee Sourdough**

**Bread Company delivered Daily.**

**Fresh Sliced Meats and Vegetables. Home Baked Chicken and Hand-Rubbed Slow Cooked Pulled Pork. Home-made Soups, Potato, Pasta and Macaroni Salads.**

**And we even Fresh-Bake our Brownies and Cookies Every Day. We will be happy to Fax you our Sandwich Menu, our Catering Menu our Hot Dog. Menu, and even our Fax Order form.**

**Full Catering Service. Free Delivery. And if it's not on our Menu...Just Ask!**

2975 Vista Blvd. Ste 101
Sparks, NV 89434
775.331.5111 Fax 775.331.5112

*Mr. Pickle*

# CLARY'S BAR & GRILL

## Buy One Drink Second is On Us!

# CLARY'S BAR & GRILL

2780 S. Virginia St.
Reno, NV 89502
775.823.9444

# Jack's Restaurant & Bar

## 2325 Kietzke Lane
## Reno, NV 89502
## 775.826.7777

**In Franktown Corners
Kietze Lane & Grove Street
Next to the carwash**

**Open 6am-4pm daily
Family owned and operated Restaurant
#1 in Quality, Service, Selection, & Prices
Specializing in Breakfast and Lunch
Full Bar**

## 2 For 1
*with purchase of two beverages*

Expires December 31, 2011

# Jack's Restaurant & Bar

# Free
## Meal Deal Upgrade
### with Wrap or Sandwich Purchase

**Anibel's**
*Dessert House & Cafe*

Expires December 31, 2011

## Anibel's Dessert House & Cafe'

### *Great Food! Awesome Bakery! Outstanding Prices!*

At Anibel's we do it all. Awesome bakery, breakfast and lunch menu, coffee, and even ice cream.
Private parties and catering also available.
Everything you need in one convenient location.
Oh yeah, did we mention our cheesecakes? Could just be the world's greatest! Our goal is your satisfaction.

We are conveniently located in the heart of Reno, just 3 blocks from Highway 395 in Franktown Corners at 2309 Kietzke Lane behind the car wash.

Phone Orders Welcome    775-82-YUMMY
775-829-8669

# ZOZO'S RISTORANTE

## FINE ITALIAN / AMERICAN DINING

### Zozo's Ristorante
### Italian/American Food
### 3446 Lakeside Dr. Reno, NV.
### 775-829-9449
### www.zozosreno.com

Enjoy regional dishes of Italy in a charming, friendly,
old world atmosphere. Daily specials, fresh fish, and seafood
& homemade desserts to make your mouth water.
Voted Best "Family Owned Italian Restaurant" in Reno.
It's where the locals have come for years.
Reservations welcome.
Visa, Mastercard & Discover

**ZOZO'S RISTORANTE**
FINE ITALIAN / AMERICAN DINING

## VALUE $6.00
## FOR DINNER ONLY
### Sunday-Thursday 4:30 to 9:00

Not valid on Friday or Saturday.
Not Valid on Sunset or Any Other Specials.

Expires December 31, 2011

We invite you to become a . . .
Partner in Education.

To become a partner or learn more about the program, contact Coleen DeLong, Partnership Coordinator, Education Alliance at 353-5533 or cdelon@washoe.k12.nv.us.
You will be partnered with a school in our district based on the needs of the school and the resources, desire and capacity of your business or service organization. We will arrange and attend a meeting with you and the school principal to get things started. Partnerships can be started at any time.

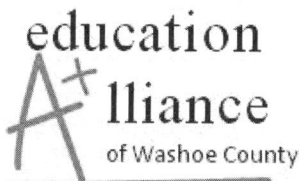

education
A⁺lliance
of Washoe County

* Support Academic Achievement in WCSD
* Provide resources and mentoring to schools and students
* Allow opportunities for your employees to be involved
* Make a positive impact on your community

## Bella Vita Catering
### "The Good Life"

Distinctive catering for
all occasions.
From an intimate evening for 2
to a festive party for 500.

Bella Vita
specializes in all the little details
that will make your event
truly successful.

**Hot & cold Appetizers** (Bruschetta, Assorted Crostini, Pesto Torta, Prawn Butter served with Baguettes)

**Soup & Salads** (Greek, Caesar, Potato, Pasta, etc)

**Sandwiches** (Meatloaf; Chicken, Egg and Tuna Salad; Turkey, etc)

**Entrees** (Seafood Paella, Fettucini Alfredo, Tri Tip served w/Tri Sauces, Chicken Chardonnay, etc)

**Sushi** (Classic raw, cooked classic rolls, customer rolls, etc)

**Desserts** (Mini Cream Puffs, Brownies, Cheesecakes, Mousse, etc)

This is just a sampling of some of the delicious menu items we offer, we are always happy to work with you on custom menus!

775-783-9475 phone / 775-783-9476 fax

# www.bellavitacateringtgl.com

# Buy One Pizza, Get 2nd Pizza
# 50% Off
## (2nd Pizza of Lesser Value)

*Pizza the Way it Oughta Be!*

**MOUNTAIN MIKE'S PIZZA**

Expires December 31, 2011

*Pizza the Way it Oughta Be!*

**MOUNTAIN MIKE'S PIZZA**

**1601 Vassar St. Reno, NV 89502**
**775-323-6060**
OR
Order ONLINE at
http://mountainmikes.besteateries.com/menu_reno.htm
We deliver to the following zip codes: 89502,
89503, 89509, 89431, 89512, 89501 & 89511

## Real Pepperoni

Mountain Mike's 'real' old world pepperoni is made using a natural casing creating a "teacup" look when cooked. Its been our signature product for over thirty years. A little crisp, a litte spicy,... Pepperoni Perfection!

## Pizzas

Small (10"), Medium (12"), Large (14"), Mountain (20")
**The Everest -** Classic Combination
**Mt. Veggiemore -** Vegetarian
**Pike's Peak -** All Meat Combo
**Robber's Roost -** Garlic Chicken Combination
**Snowy Alps -** Garlic Combo
**Pineapple Chicken Luau -** Grilled Chicken & Dole Pineapple
**Chicken Club -** Better than a BLT
**Sizzlin' Bacon Classic -** A family favorite!
**Garlic Tuscan -** A frenzy for your taste buds!
**Diamond Head -** Ham and Dole pineapple
**Mt. St. Helen's -** A flavor explosion!

## Sandwiches

### Half Dome
An open-faced pizza sandwich with pizza sauce, mozzarella cheese and your choice of up to three pizza toppings. Served with pickle and chips.

### Cliff Hanger
A fresh roll loaded with your choice of chicken, salami, ham, Louisiana-style Hot Sausage or Canadian Style Bacon, crisp lettuce, fresh tomato and your choice of cheese - Served with pickle and chips.

### Appetizers & Sides
Garlic Bread-*plain or with cheese,*
Garlic Sticks-*plain or with cheese,*
Hot Wings, Chicken Bites
Mozzarella Sticks, Jalapeño Poppers

INDIAN GARDEN
Offers beautiful décor,
friendly staff and the
finest cuisine to guarantee
an evening to remember.

## INDIAN GARDEN
Multi Cuisine Restaurant
Endless tepmtation

1565 So. Virginia St Reno, NV 89509   775-337-8002 or 775-337-8003

### Hot Appetizers

Meat Samosa - light spicy turnovers stuffed with minced lamb & spices
Spring Roll – mixed vegetables sauteed, rolled and deep fried
Fish Pakora – pieces of fresh swordfish deep fried in chickpea batter

### Curry Dishes

Boneless chicken or fish cooked in thick curry sauce and garnished with fresh Coriander
Lamb or beef cubes cooked in thick gravy of exotic spices and herbs

### Vindaloo

A SPECIALTY OF GOA!! Lamb pieces marinated in vinegar and spices, cooked with potatoes
in a spicy tomato and onion sauce.
Also available in chicken, beef and fish variations!

### Rogan Josh

A SPECIALTY OF DISH OF KASHMIR, lean lamb pieces cooked in  yogurt, almonds and a
blend of fragrant spices.

### Tandoori Specialties, Rice Specialties and India Breads

Items like Tandoori Tika, Lamb Biryani, Punjabi Paratha and Aloo Naan

### Large Vegetarian Menu!

Over 15 different vegetarian items to choose from plus appetizers!

**Dine In or To Go-- Free Delivery within 5 miles** (with minimum order of $30)

Get the WHOLE NINE YARDS

**LAMPPOST PIZZA**

EST 1976

At Your Neighborhood Pizzeria
**& Sports Bar**

We have Fresh Hand-Tossed Pizza
Delicious Salads, Sandwiches, Pastas and MORE!

- Daily Specials
- Lunch Specials
- Take-N-Bake
- Party Menu
- Neighborly Bar
- On-Line Ordering
- Party Reservations
- Family Karaoke Fridays
- Game Room for All Ages
- Dine In/Carry Out/Delivery

## Call NOW or Go Online to Order!
## 775-853-7887
## www.LamppostPizzaReno.com

1141 Steamboat Pkwy #930 Reno, NV 89521 (RC Willey Center)
Follow us On Twitter: @lamppostpizza
Or Facebook: LamppostPizza Reno

**Buy 1 Meal and 2 Drinks**
**Get a 2nd Meal FREE**
*(of equal or lesser value)*

Expires December 31, 2011

293

# Sushi Club

## The Best Place For The Best Sushi

### All You Can Eat!

$1.50 off All You Can Eat Lunch and Dinner
Monday-Thursday must present this offer

Eat Free on your birthday with parties of 6 or more

Create Your Own Roll, Signature Cocktails,
Party Platters, Delivery & Carry Out
294 E. Moana Lane  Reno, NV 89509  775.828.7311

## *Happy Hour Special*
## *3:00-5:30: $15.95*
## *All You Can Eat Dinner*

Expires December 31, 2011

Sushi Club

# 2 Topping deLITE®
# $5.99

## Papa Murphy's
### TAKE 'N' BAKE PIZZA

940 W. Moana Lane #108
Reno, Nevada • 775-826-8767
Expires December 31, 2011

940 W. Moana Lane #108 • Reno, Nevada 89509 • 775-826-8767

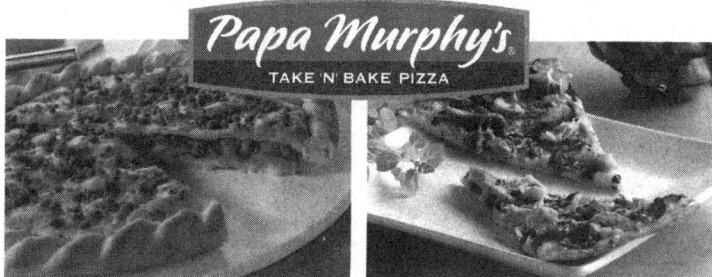

## Papa Murphy's
### TAKE 'N' BAKE PIZZA

### Signature Pizzas
*Your Favorite Pizzas Featuring our Very Own Traditional Pizza Sauce. Exclusively at Papa Murphy's.*

| | Medium | Large | Family |
|---|---|---|---|
| Murphy's Combination | 12.99 | 14.99 | 15.99 |

Salami, Pepperoni, Italian Sausage, Mushrooms, Onions, Black Olives

| The Cowboy | 12.99 | 14.99 | 15.99 |
|---|---|---|---|

Pepperoni, Italian Sausage, Mushrooms, Black Olives, Herb & Cheese Blend

| Papa's Favorite | 12.99 | 14.99 | 15.99 |
|---|---|---|---|

Pepperoni, Italian Sausage, Ground Beef, Mushrooms, Mixed Onions, Green Peppers, Black Olives

| Papa's All Meat | 12.99 | 14.99 | 15.99 |
|---|---|---|---|

Canadian Bacon, Salami, Pepperoni, Italian Sausage, Ground Beef

| The Vegetarian | 12.99 | 14.99 | 15.99 |
|---|---|---|---|

Mushrooms, Mixed Onions, Green Peppers, Black Olives, Roma Tomatoes

| Papa's Perfect Pizza | 10.99 | 11.99 | 12.99 |
|---|---|---|---|

1/2 Pepperoni, 1/2 Hawaiian Pizza

| The Hawaiian | 10.99 | 11.99 | 12.99 |
|---|---|---|---|

Canadian Bacon and Pineapple

| Pepperoni | 9.99 | 10.99 | 11.99 |
|---|---|---|---|

### Stuffed Pizzas
*Two Layers of Dough Stuffed With Your Favorite Toppings.*

| | Large | Family |
|---|---|---|
| 5-Meat Stuffed™ | 15.99 | 16.99 |

Canadian Bacon, Pepperoni, Italian Sausage, Crispy Bacon, Ground Beef, Traditional Pizza Sauce, Mozzarella Cheese

| Chicago-Style Stuffed™ | 15.99 | 16.99 |
|---|---|---|

Salami, Pepperoni, Italian Sausage, Ground Beef, Onions, Roma Tomatoes, Traditional Pizza Sauce, Mozzarella Cheese

| Chicken & Bacon Stuffed™ | 15.99 | 16.99 |
|---|---|---|

Creamy Garlic Sauce, Grilled Chicken, Crispy Bacon, Roma Tomatoes, Onions, Mozzarella Cheese

### Gourmet Pizzas
*Our Creamy Garlic Sauce and the Freshest, Highest Quality Toppings.*

| | Medium | Large | Family |
|---|---|---|---|
| Gourmet Chicken Garlic | 12.99 | 14.99 | 15.99 |

Grilled Chicken, Roma Tomatoes, Green Onions, Herb & Cheese Blend

| Gourmet Vegetarian | 12.99 | 14.99 | 15.99 |
|---|---|---|---|

Spinach, Zucchini, Mushrooms, Marinated Artichoke Hearts, Roma Tomatoes, Onions, Herb & Cheese Blend

| Gourmet Classic Italian | 12.99 | 14.99 | 15.99 |
|---|---|---|---|

Pepperoni, Italian Sausage, Mushrooms, Roma Tomatoes, Green Onions, Herb & Cheese Blend

### Thin Crust deLITE®
*Our Exclusive Crispy Thin Crust. Same Great Taste – 40% Fewer Calories, 30% Less Fat.*
*\*Compared to the equivalent Original Crust Pizza.*

| | Large |
|---|---|
| Chicken Bacon Artichoke deLITE® | 11.99 |

Creamy Garlic Sauce, Grilled Chicken, Crispy Bacon, Marinated Artichoke Hearts, Spinach, Parmesan Cheese

| Herb Chicken Mediterranean deLITE® | 11.99 |
|---|---|

Olive Oil, Garlic, Mozzarella Cheese, Spinach, Grilled Chicken, Sun-Dried Tomatoes, Feta Cheese

| Veggie deLITE® | 10.99 |
|---|---|

Creamy Garlic Sauce, Spinach, Mushrooms, Roma Tomatoes

| Meat deLITE® | 10.99 |
|---|---|

Pepperoni, Italian Sausage, Ground Beef

| 2-Topping deLITE® | 9.99 |
|---|---|

Our Exclusive Crispy Thin Crust with 2 of your favorite toppings

| Pepperoni deLITE® | 8.99 |
|---|---|
| Cheese deLITE® | 7.99 |

### Custom Pizzas

### Side Items

## Lots More!

295

# THA JOINT

Business Hours:
Mon-Sat
11:00 –9:00
Sun 12:30-9:00

775.626.8677

**thajointsushi.com**

## ALL YOU CAN EAT SUSHI BAR & GRILL
## MENU, KOREAN GRILL, SUSHI

Appetizers, Nigiri Sushi, Maki Sushi/Hand Rolls,
Vegetarian Rolls/Hand Rolls.

*Join our FACEBOOK FAN PAGE!*

---

**Truckee River Bar & Grill**

*Ask about the Local's Discount Guide Special*

Expires December 31, 2011

# Truckee River Bar & Grill
# 3466 Lakeside Dr.
# Reno, NV 89509
# 825.5585

Hours of Operation: 5:30 AM to 7 PM • 6 AM to 6 PM Saturday & Sunday

# JOLT-N-JAVA

Coffee, Breakfast and Sandwiches, Ice Cream

The Best Deal
in Spanish Springs

Locally Owned

Friendly Employees

Best Selection & Service

Best Quality Coffee
from High Sierra Coffee
Roastery

Best Neighborhood Shop

Drive Thru Service Also!

## (775) 354-2121

Location: 5255 Vista Blvd • Sparks, NV • Vista and N. Los Altos

**Buy One Drink or Sandwich,**
# Get One FREE
**(or 50% Off Single Sandwich or Drink Purchase)**

JOLT-N-JAVA

Expires December 31, 2011

Jim Boy's
Tacos

*Buy One Taco or Burrito with a Drink
and Get One Similar Item
of equal or lesser value FREE.*

Expires December 31, 2011

# Jim Boy's Tacos
# 1999 Selmi Dr
# Reno, NV 89512
# 775.284.8208

# Si Amigos Mexican Restaurant
# 1553 S. Virginia St.
# Reno, NV 89502
# 775.348.1445

$9.99 Large 1 Topping Pizza and $19.99 Family Special: Large 1 Topping Pizza, Breadsticks and Wings.

Expires December 31, 2011

# Voted BEST Pizza

## Pizza & Pub

| 834 Victorian Ave | 6405 S. Virginia St. |
| Sparks, NV | Reno, NV |
| 775.351.2000 | 775.284.8900 |

## www.BlindOnion.com

## zpizza

# 3600 Warren Way Suite 101
# Reno, NV 89509

Phone Number: 775-828-6565
Business Hours: 11:00 am – 9:30 pm (Mon-Sun)
www.zpizza.com

*Dine in*      *Delivery*      *Take out*
*Organic*      *Vegan*       *Gluten Free*

# $5 Off
## Any Size Pizza
*Coupon valid at above location only.*
Expires December 31, 2011

zpizza

**LOCAL'S DISCOUNT GUIDE**

*Little*
**PHILADELPHIA**
*Cheesesteaks*

Philadelphia Cheesesteak
2755 Kietzke Ln.
Reno, NV 89502
775.825.8488

**LOCAL'S DISCOUNT GUIDE**

# Haven on Earth
# Bread & Bakery Co.
### The ONLY 100% Gluten-Free Bakery in the region.

Haven On Earth
10855 Double R. Blvd Ste A
Reno, NV 89521
284.4200

**LOCAL'S DISCOUNT GUIDE**

# $2 PBR All the Time, 1st Beer Free
### with coupon

Victorian Saloon
908 Victorian Ave
Sparks, NV
560.5656

# Victorian Saloon
## 908 Victorian Ave
## Sparks, NV

Expires December 31, 2011

---

**LOCAL'S DISCOUNT GUIDE**

# $1.00 Off
## Purchase of Any
## Large Size Menu Item

TCBY The Country's Best Yogurt

Buy One Large Size Menu Item
Get $1.00 Off!

The Best Frozen Treat
You Can Buy!

Valid Only at 900 W. Moana Ln
Not Valid with Any Other Offer

HOURS: 11 am-9 pm Daily

Expires December 31, 2011

# TCBY®
### The Country's Best Yogurt

**LOCAL'S DISCOUNT GUIDE**

Victorian Saloon
908 Victorian Ave
Sparks, NV
560.5656

**LOCAL'S DISCOUNT GUIDE**

## TCBY®
The Country's Best Yogurt

TCBY
900 W. Moana Ln
At Lakeside Crossing
Lakeside & Moana
Reno, NV 89509
829.7447

* All offers of 2 for 1 or Buy 1 Get 1 are good on equal or lesser valued items only.

**LOCAL'S DISCOUNT GUIDE**

# Buy 1, Get the 2nd
# 50% off

Thai Lotus Restaurant
6430 Ste#A
South Virginia Street
Reno, NV 89511
Tel: 775.852.5033
www.thailotusreno.com

Business Hours:
Mon-Fri 11:00-3:00, 5:00-9:00
Sat 11:00-21:00
Sunday closed.

**Thai Lotus**
Thai Lotus Thai Cuisine

Expires December 31, 2011

---

* All offers of 2 for 1 or Buy 1 Get 1 are good on equal or lesser valued items only.

**LOCAL'S DISCOUNT GUIDE**

# $2 Off
## $10 or More

Don Juan's Bakery
113 Los Altos Pkwy #708
Sparks, NV 89436
775.626.8119

HOURS: Mon-Fri 7 am-8pm,
Sat-Sun 7 am-5 pm

*Don Juan's Bakery*

Expires December 31, 2011

**LOCAL'S DISCOUNT GUIDE**

*Thai Lotus*
Thai Lotus Thai Cuisine

Thai Lotus
6430 So. Virginia St. Ste #A
Reno, NV 89511
775.772.1449

**LOCAL'S DISCOUNT GUIDE**

*Don Juan's Bakery*

Don Juan's Bakery
113 Los Altos Pkwy #708
Sparks, NV 89436
626.8119

## LOCAL'S DISCOUNT GUIDE

### Red Dog Saloon
Bar – Pizza – Music

Red Dog Saloon
76 No. C Street
Virginia City, NV 89440
775.847.7474

## LOCAL'S DISCOUNT GUIDE

Jazz, A Louisiana Kitchen
1180 Scheels Dr. Ste B-111
Sparks, NV 89434
657.8659

**LOCAL'S DISCOUNT GUIDE**

## Buy One Meal
# Get One Free
### Of Equal or Lesser Value (Excludes Lasagna)
### One meal per coupon. Valid on Mon-Tues Only

Serving Reno Since 1937

Casale's Halfway Club
2501 E. 4th Street
Reno, NV 89502
775.323.3979

HOURS: 11:30 am-9 pm

# Casale's
# Halfway Club

### Serving Reno since 1937

Expires December 31, 2011

---

We invite you to become a . . .
Partner in Education.

To become a partner or learn more about the program, contact Coleen DeLong Partnership Coordinator, Education Alliance at 353-5533 or cdelon@washoe.k12.nv.us.
You will be partnered with a school in our district based on the needs of the school and the resources, desire and capacity of your business or service organization. We will arrange and attend a meeting with you and the school principal to get things started. Partnerships can be started at any time.

## education
## A⁺lliance
### of Washoe County

* Support Academic Achievement in WCSD
* Provide resources and mentoring to schools and students
* Allow opportunities for your employees to be involved
* Make a positive impact on your community

**LOCAL'S DISCOUNT GUIDE**

Casale's Halfway Club
2501 E. 4th Street
Reno, NV 89502
775.323.3979

We invite you to become a...
Partner in Education.

To become a partner or learn more about the program, contact Coleen DeLong, Partnership Coordinator, Education Alliance at 353-5533 or cdelon@washoe.k12.nv.us.
You will be partnered with a school in our district based on the needs of the school and the resources, desire and capacity of your business or service organization. We will arrange and attend a meeting with you and the school principal to get things started. Partnerships can be started at any time.

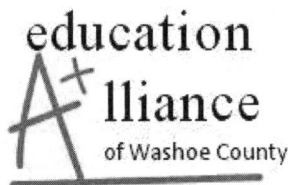

**education A+lliance**
of Washoe County

* Support Academic Achievement in WCSD
* Provide resources and mentoring to schools and students
* Allow opportunities for your employees to be involved
* Make a positive impact on your community

# DINING

## My Favorite Muffin & Bagel Cafe

• Muffins and Bagels baked fresh daily! • Sandwiches
• Smoothies • Salads & Soup • Coffee & Espresso
• Party Platters • Gift Baskets • Free WiFi®

**South Downtown***
**340 California Ave.**
**(775) 333-1025**

**Shoppers Square**
**259 E. Plumb Ln**
**(775) 333-6536**

**D'Andrea Marketplace***
**2868 Vista Blvd**
**(Sparks)**
**(775) 351-2868**

## Buy ANY Sandwich, Get 2nd Sandwich
# 50% Off (ELV)

Not valid with any other special or discount.
Valid only at locations noted. Exp. 12/31/11

### LOCAL'S DISCOUNT GUIDE

Expires December 31, 2011

---

### LOCAL'S DISCOUNT GUIDE

## *Buy One Regular Plate and a Beverage*
# *Get One Mini Plate FREE*

L&L Hawaiian Barbecue

4991 S. Virginia St. Unit B
Reno, NV 89502
775-677-8888

295 Los Altos Pkwy #101
Sparks, NV 89436
775-829-9888

**L&L**
Hawaiian Barbecue
SINCE 1976 *Hawaii* ®

Expires December 31, 2011

## Local's Discount Guide

### My Favorite Muffin & Bagel Cafe

| | | |
|---|---|---|
| 340 California Ave | 259 E. Plumb Ln | 2868 Vista Blvd |
| South Downtown | Shoppers Square | D'Andrea Marketplace |
| Reno, NV | Reno, NV | Sparks, NV |
| (775) 333-1025 | (775) 333-6536 | (775) 351-2868 |

Offer validity is governed by the Rules of Use and excludes defined holidays. Offers are not valid with other discount offers unless specified. Coupons void if purchased, sold or bartered. Discounts exclude tax, tip and/or alcohol, where applicable.

## Local's Discount Guide

### L&L Hawaiian Barbecue

| | |
|---|---|
| 4991 S. Virginia St. Unit B | 295 Los Altos Pkwy #101 |
| Reno, NV 89502 | Sparks, NV 89436 |
| 775.677.8888 | 775.829.9888 |

Offer validity is governed by the Rules of Use and excludes defined holidays. Offers are not valid with other discount offers unless specified. Coupons void if purchased, sold or bartered. Discounts exclude tax, tip and/or alcohol, where applicable.

**LOCAL'S DISCOUNT GUIDE**

# 15% Off
## Any Order of $20 or More

Serving Reno/Sparks Area
Since 1986

Dine-In, Take-Out, Full Bar

Come to Try Our Authentic
Chinese Menu

HOURS:
Sun-Fri 11 am-2:30 pm,
4:30 pm-9 pm

# Szechuan Garden

Expires December 31, 2011

**LOCAL'S DISCOUNT GUIDE**

## Buy Any Item $7.95 or Less
## Get One Item of Equal
## or Lesser Value Free
**Not valid with any other offers, discounts or
coupons. Has no cash value.**

Sneakers Bar & Grill
P.O. Box 10236
Reno, NV 89570
775.223.5488

# SNEAKERS
## BAR & GRILL

# Sneakers Bar & Grill

Expires December 31, 2011

## DINING

**LOCAL'S DISCOUNT GUIDE**

錦川 Szechuan Garden

Szechuan Garden
903 W. Moana Ln
Reno, NV 89509
775.827.6333

**LOCAL'S DISCOUNT GUIDE**

**SNEAKERS BAR & GRILL**

Sneakers Bar & Grill
P.O. Box 10236
Reno, NV 89570
775.223.5488

# DINING

### Yellow Submarine
920 Holman Way
Sparks, NV 89431
775.358.6040

### InkBerry Breakfast House
400 W. 5th St. Suite 104
Reno, NV 89521
775.338.9263

We invite you to become a . . .
Partner in Education.

To become a partner or learn more about the program, contact Coleen DeLong, Partnership Coordinator, Education Alliance at 353-5533 or cdelon@washoe.k12.nv.us.
You will be partnered with a school in our district based on the needs of the school and the resources, desire and capacity of your business or service organization. We will arrange and attend a meeting with you and the school principal to get things started. Partnerships can be started at any time.

# education
# A+ lliance
### of Washoe County

*Support Academic Achievement in WCSD
*Provide resources and mentoring to schools and students
*Allow opportunities for your employees to be involved
*Make a positive impact on your community

We invite you to become a . . .
Partner in Education.

To become a partner or learn more
about the program, contact Coleen
DeLong, Partnership Coordinator,
Education Alliance at 353-5533 or
cdelon@washoe.k12.nv.us.
You will be partnered with a school in
our district based on the needs of the
school and the resources, desire and
capacity of your business or service
organization. We will arrange and
attend a meeting with you and the
school principal to get things started.
Partnerships can be started at any time.

**education
A+ lliance**
of Washoe County

* Support Academic Achievement in
WCSD
* Provide resources and mentoring to
schools and students
* Allow opportunities for your employees to
be involved
* Make a positive impact on your
community

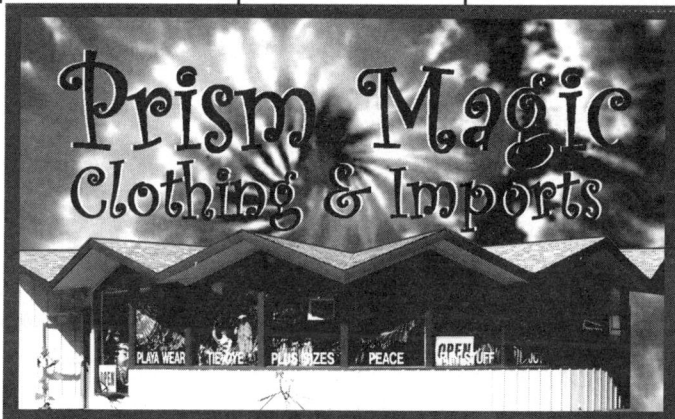

**Reno's Only Create Your Own Candle Studio**

# Flicker

## Create Your Own Candles

*Everyone is welcome. Weekdays or weekends...with family or friends.*

Come into our relaxing studio & create a one of a kind luminary, candlescape or chunk mosaic candle. Choose from a large selection of molds, colors, fragrances & specialty shapes.

Candle prices start at just $12.

- Parties for Kids & Adults
- Wine & Candle Making
- Girls Night Out
- Date Night
- Bridal & Baby Showers

**3594 W. Plumb Lane - Reno**
**775-324-GLOW**
**www.flickerreno.com**

Hours:
Mon & Thurs 10a-6p
Fri & Sat 10a-7p
Sun 11a-4p

# His WORD
A PARABLE CHRISTIAN STORE

# 20% Off
## Any Nonsale Book

Expires December 31, 2011

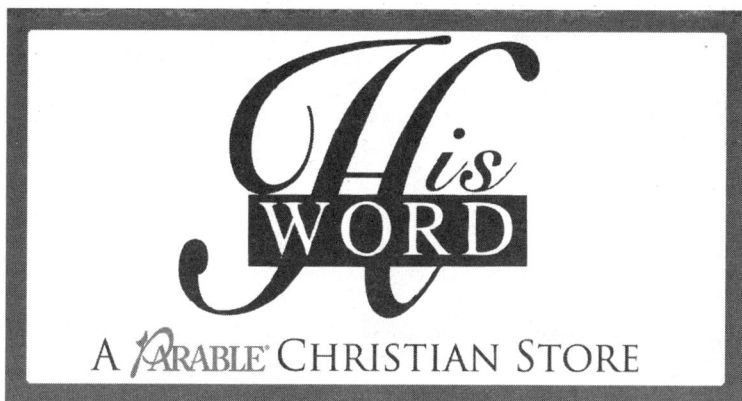

# His WORD
## A PARABLE CHRISTIAN STORE

### Two locations to serve you

| | |
|---|---|
| 7689 S Virginia | 810 Holman Way |
| Longley West Plaza | Pyramid Shopping Center |
| 853-2665 | 359-7940 |

**www.parable.com**
Hours: 10am to 8pm Monday to Friday
and 10am to 6pm Saturday

# Sprint®

## STORE HOURS:

Mon-Fri: 10 am to 8 pm
Sat: 10 am to 7 pm
Sun: 12 pm to 5 pm

## STORE LOCATIONS:

| | | |
|---|---|---|
| 1565 E. Lincoln Way #R103 | 173 Los Altos Pkwy | 2870 Northtowne Ln #105 |
| Sparks, NV 89436 | Sparks, NV 89436 | Reno, NV 89436 |
| 775-359-4300 | 775-626-7300 | 775-359-3002 |

324

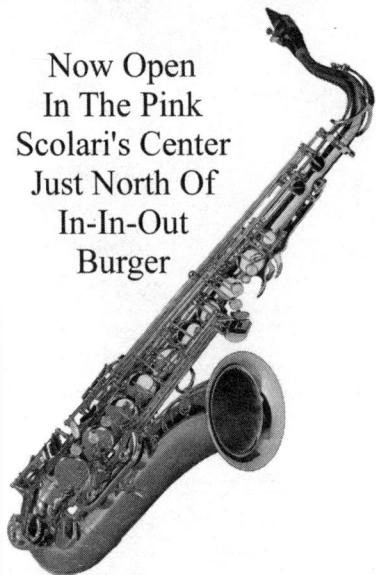

# *Happy Song Gift Baskets*

# *10% Off*
## *Your First Order*

## *Happy Song Gift Baskets*
**Baskets for Everyone, Business & All Ages**

### 🎵 *Happy Song* 🎵

A song is an instant mental escape to another time or place; a place to put your problems behind you and just enjoy the moment. A pleasant, happy song causes smiles, warm feelings, and well wishes. Our personalized *Happy Song Gift Baskets* are designed with just that in mind. We will gladly make your basket(s) with any theme you deem appropriate, with special items you suggest, and to your personal specifications. *Contact us today and put that "Happy Song" in someone's heart.*

*We proudly use products from locally owned businesses only. Local money spent locally will circulate three times among all of us.*

## Phone: (775) 379-6904
## Email: linduh1956@gmail.com

# live beautifully

At G.J. Rhodes, *you will find the most luxurious personal care items and the finest selection of candles for your home.*

*Fine shopping in Reno is a reality at G.J. Rhodes.*

**G.J. RHODES**
FOR THE HOME

**3400 Lakeside Drive, Reno**
in the Moana West Shopping Center
**775.825.4100**

give beautifully

328

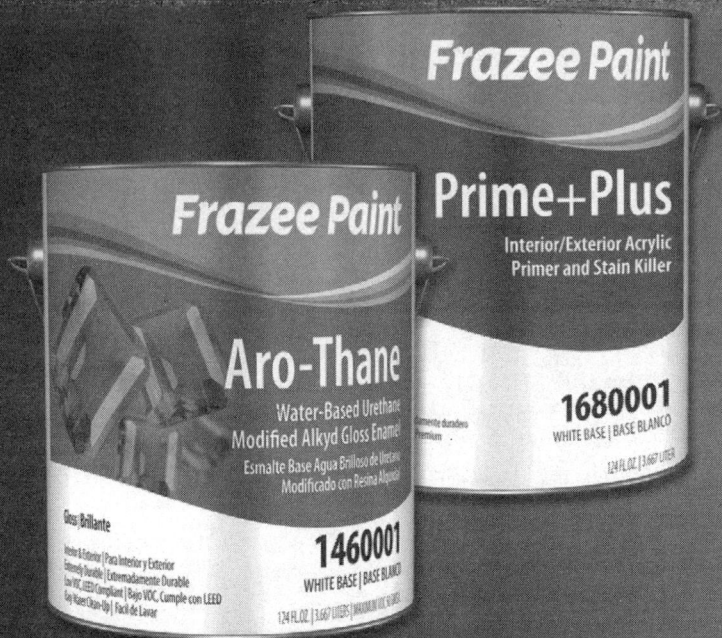
330

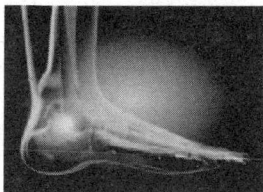

# 10% Discount
## on Orthotics & Footwear

Expires December 31, 2011

**Specialty Footwear & Orthotics**
113 Los Altos Parkway, Suite #104
Sparks, NV 89436

Website: specialtyfootwearsparks.com

Phone: 775-741-3396
specialtyfootwear@charter.net

**10% DISCOUNT on Orthotics & Footwear**

"YOUR SHOE & ORTHOTIC EXPERTS"

*Peter Padilla, C.Ped*

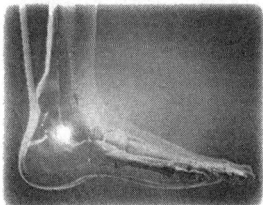

- *Extra Depth/Width Shoes* •
- *Custom Orthotics* •
- *Shoe Modifications* •
- *Expert Fitting* •
- *Custom Made Shoes* •

Phone: **775-741-3396**          113 Los Altos Parkway, Suite #104
specialtyfootwear@charter.net                    Sparks, NV 89436

331

# FAIRWAY MOTORS

## ONE WAY ... Your Way!

### 940 S. Virginia St. Reno, Nevada
### 775.348.0505

FAIRWAY MOTORS

## One Year of
## Free Oil Changes
## with a New Filter.
**With purchase of vehicle from Fairway Motors.
Limit 4 per year - once every 3 months.**

Expires December 31, 2011

# See Below
## For Special Offers

American Furniture & Mattress Inc

Expires December 31, 2011    1633 Prater Way, Sparks, NV 89436 • 775.355.8899

We invite you to become a . . .
Partner in Education.

To become a partner or learn more about the program, contact Coleen DeLong, Partnership Coordinator, Education Alliance at 353-5533 or cdelon@washoe.k12.nv.us. You will be partnered with a school in our district based on the needs of the school and the resources, desire and capacity of your business or service organization. We will arrange and attend a meeting with you and the school principal to get things started. Partnerships can be started at any time.

# education
# A⁺lliance
### of Washoe County

\* Support Academic Achievement in WCSD
\* Provide resources and mentoring to schools and students
\* Allow opportunities for your employees to be involved
\* Make a positive impact on your community

**FASTFRAME**
EXPERT PICTURE FRAMING

Expires December 31, 2011

## 20% OFF
*Gift Certificate*

Present this certificate and receive
20% off your custom framing order.

**FASTFRAME**
EXPERT PICTURE FRAMING

Design & Craftsmanship, Your Total Satisfaction Guarantee.

Must present coupon when ordering. Limit one coupon per
household. Offer good for custom framing orders only. Not valid
with any other offer. Not valid on work in progress.

RENO
940 W. MOANA LN # 103
825-4499

*accent your life*

Our creative designers can help you get
just the right look that will complement
your furnishings, your lifestyle, and your
home. Let us capture your favorite art,
photos, or memorabilia in a custom
crafted frame you'll treasure for a lifetime.

*Voted Reno's Best Frame Shop*

## 940 W Moana Ln # 103
## 825-4499

*Our everyday prices beat the so called 50% off sales!*

**FASTFRAME**
EXPERT PICTURE FRAMING

*Design & Craftsmanship,
Your Total Satisfaction Guarantee.*

# EL TAPATIO MARKET

- Piniatas
- Mexican Candy
- Mexican Dried Spices
  for Every Need
- Phone Cards
- Mexican Groceries
- Liquor & Beer Low Prices
- Cigarettes
- Candles
- Incense
- Roseries
- Mexican Socks

*Spanish & English*

347 S. Wells, Reno, NV 89502 • 775.322.6111

# Free
## Roller Cover
**with purchase of Gallon of Paint**

Expires December 31, 2011

## Fuller Color Center

HOURS: Mon-Fri 7 am-5 pm,
Sat 8 am-3 pm, Closed Sun

# Fuller Color Center
# 75 S. Wells Ave
# Reno, NV 89502
# 329.4478

the **niche**
clothing & home decor

**RENO**
next to costco
1300 e. plumb ln.
775.348.8661

**SPARKS**
galleria mall
121 los altos pkwy
775.626.8820

**TRUCKEE**
10164 donner pass rd
530.587.3100

JOIN THE PARTY @ SHOPTHENICHE.COM & FACEBOOK

1 item per coupon, one coupon per customer, not valid with any other offer.

# HORSESHOE
## JEWELRY AND LOAN

## *25% Off*
## *All Jewelry Repair*

www.jewelryman.com

# HORSESHOE
## JEWELRY AND LOAN

# www.jewelryman.com

Horseshoe Jewelry & Loan
229 N. Virginia St.
Reno, NV 89501
323.4554

# Dylan's Bear Factory & More

## 775-379-6904
### Email: linduh1956@gmail.com

Here at Dylan's Bear Factory & More,
when we say "More" that is really what we mean.
We offer unique, one of a kind, hand designed and sewn
Teddy Bears from play size to collectible miniatures.
Pick your personal preference of style, colors, and size.
We also have sewing solutions from doll clothes to
curtains or pillowcases and offering classes.
Call us with your ideas today.

## 10% Off
### Your Order or Total Class Including Supplies

*Dylan's Bear Factory & More*

Expires December 31, 2011

340

**LOCAL'S
DISCOUNT
GUIDE**

High Desert Pool & Spa
3470 Lakeside Dr.
Reno, NV 89509
775.329.9299

**LOCAL'S
DISCOUNT
GUIDE**

# SPRING
## IN YOUR STEP

Spring in Your Step
3 N. Virginia St
Reno, NV 89501
337.0333

**LOCAL'S DISCOUNT GUIDE**

# 5% Discount
## On Purchase of Over $30

Make shopping fun again!
Shop your Bargain Market
and Save!
Return this for a 5% discount on a
purchase over $30!
You're already a winner!

HOURS: Mon-Sun, 8 am-8 pm

**GROCERY OUTLET**
*bargain market*™

Expires December 31, 2011

---

**LOCAL'S DISCOUNT GUIDE**

# 15% Off
## Total Order

All Things Nevada!
Come check out our custom
Nevada shaped gift baskets and
pure, unprocessed local honey!

HOURS: Mon-Fri 9:30 am-5:30,
Sat 10 am-4 pm, Sun: CLOSED

THE NEVADA STORE

Expires December 31, 2011

**GROCERY OUTLET**
bargain market™

Grocery Outlet
3800 Kietzke Ln #130
Reno, NV 89502
775.826.7688

THE NEVADA STORE

The Nevada Store
3368 Lakeside Ct.
Reno, NV 89509
775.825.3318

We invite you to become a . . .
Partner in Education.

To become a partner or learn more about the program, contact Coleen DeLong, Partnership Coordinator, Education Alliance at 353-5533 or cdelon@washoe.k12.nv.us. You will be partnered with a school in our district based on the needs of the school and the resources, desire and capacity of your business or service organization. We will arrange and attend a meeting with you and the school principal to get things started. Partnerships can be started at any time.

education
A+lliance
of Washoe County

* Support Academic Achievement in WCSD
* Provide resources and mentoring to schools and students
* Allow opportunities for your employees to be involved
* Make a positive impact on your community

We invite you to become a...
Partner in Education.

To become a partner or learn more about the program, contact Coleen DeLong, Partnership Coordinator, Education Alliance at 353-5533 or cdelon@washoe.k12.nv.us.
You will be partnered with a school in our district based on the needs of the school and the resources, desire and capacity of your business or service organization. We will arrange and attend a meeting with you and the school principal to get things started. Partnerships can be started at any time.

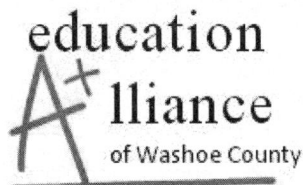

# education
## A+lliance
of Washoe County

* Support Academic Achievement in WCSD
* Provide resources and mentoring to schools and students
* Allow opportunities for your employees to be involved
* Make a positive impact on your community

🐾 **REIGNING CATS & DOGS** 🐾

# 20% OFF*

## SUPPLIES

*Not valid for cat or dog food.*
Must present coupon. Expires 12/31/11

**1338 Disc Drive**
**Sparks, NV**
**(775) 626-3433**

🐾 **FOOD & SUPPLIES FOR ALL PETS** 🐾

Expires December 31, 2011

---

**LOCAL'S DISCOUNT GUIDE**

# 10% Off
## with coupon

# TIMELESS
# TREASURES

Located at the Lafayette Market

HOURS: 7 Days a Week 9-5

Expires December 31, 2011

**LOCAL'S DISCOUNT GUIDE**

Reigning Cats & Dogs
1338 Disc Drive
Sparks, NV 89436
775.626.3433

**LOCAL'S DISCOUNT GUIDE**

# TIMELESS TREASURES

Timeless Treasures
66 No. C Street
Virginia City, NV 89440
775.847.7742

## LEE'S Janitorial Services
"WE CATER TO YOUR NEEDS!"

Expires December 31, 2011

**Ask about our Realtor's Advantage Discount**

## LEE'S Janitorial Services
"WE CATER TO YOUR NEEDS!"

Lee's Janitorial Services guarantees all our work, if there should be a problem, just give us a call and we will take care of it within 48 hours at no additional cost to you.

SOME of our services.....
- Office Cleaning
- Windows
- Floors - Stripped & waxed
- Move Outs
- Handyman Services
- And much more!

# WE CATER TO YOUR NEEDS!

**Family Owned and Operated for more than 25 years.**

www.leesjanitorial.com

# (530) 368-1802

Licensed
Insured
Bonded

## NO JOB TOO SMALL

### Top Notch
# Handyman Services

**Alan Lynch:** *Licensed Specialist*

# 775-722-2526

## *Folks, make sure your handyman is LICENSED!!*

I am a LICENSED handyman with over 30 years experience, and will do anything you need done. From fence repair to taking down Christman lights to hanging ceiling fans to walking your dog. Hauling, carpentry, plumbing, electrical, flooring, painting, concrete, roofing, etc. NO JOB TOO SMALL! $25/hr. - 2 hr. minimum. Give me a call and I'll come see what you got. I also have the ability and manpower to do remodels and additions. References upon request.

### Top Notch Handyman Services
### 775-722-2526
### License: 036852

# 20% Off
## Any Handy Man Service

### Top Notch
# Handyman Services

Expires December 31, 2011

353

# Dance City Dance Academy

DCDA has classes for all ages. We specialize in Ballet, Jazz, Hip Hop, Contemporary, Lyrical and Ballroom. We have the most highly qualified and talented staff to teach you all the best moves.

Dance City Dance Academy and Events Center
Book that next special event at Dance City.
Weddings, Birthdays, Office Party Etc.
Call for details.

5318 Sparks Blvd.
Sparks, NV 89436
775-626-4457
dancecitysparks.com

# It's Time to Get Your Dance On!

*Present this coupon and come to any one class*
*of your choice for FREE*
*(Call or go online for class schedule)*

Dance Academy

Expires December 31, 2011

# Marx Video Service
## 25th Anniversary

# 50% Off
## Initial Trip Charge or First Hour of Service

Expires December 31, 2011

**Marx**
**VIDEO**
*Service*
(Est. 1985)

## 25th Anniversary!

## 3454 Lakeside Dr
## Reno, NV 89509
## 775-827-3222

Design, sales & installation of home theatre and video observation.

*"Our certified video technician is a factory authorized repair agent, not just an installer!"*

- We still offer complete service and repair of all video products.

- We can "clean up" previously installed systems.

- We can diagnose problems and upgrade systems if needed.

- We are offering a 50% discount off initial trip charge or first hour of service.

# $5 Off
## Minimum $25
### Order Wash Dry Fold Drop

Must present coupon upon drop off service.
Limit 1 coupon per customer.

**DUDS'n SUDS**
*Good clean fun !*

Expires December 31, 2011

# Duds N Suds
## *Fully Attended Laundry*

HOURS:
Mon-Fri 7 am-5 pm
Sat 8 am-3 pm
Closed Sun

# We Make Laundry Fun
# Direct TV & Wi Fi Available
# Snack Bar & Beer

# A1 Moving

**Worry Free/Stress Free Move**
**Over 20 Years Experience**
**Local, Reliable & Dependable**

**We Take Care of Your Stuff**
**BETTER Than You Would**

**No Job Too Big or Too Small**

## 15% Off
### Total Move

Expires December 31, 2011

## A1 Moving

P.O. Box 40491
Reno, NV 89505
775.342.4289

For more information, or for your custom quote please contact
**Sara Ashley**
**Cabinet Ink**
**(775)622-9896**
**Sashley@childrenscabinet.org**
**Business hours 9am to 6pm**
**Located at 777 Sinclair St. Reno, Nv 89501**

Expires December 31, 2011

## UNLIKE ANY OTHER PRINT SHOP...

**Cabinet Ink was established to provide working
opportunities for at-risk youth, while learning the
value of working in a business environment, as
well as teaching them a marketable skill and a
valuable trade they can use for a lifetime. The youth
are able to see their accomplishments and hard
work materialize through Cabinet Ink.**

**All proceeds support the youth of Cabinet Ink**

The **Children's**
**Cabinet**

# Jimmy's EXPRESS CARWASH & QUICK LUBE

## 10170 N. McCarran

VISA MasterCard **747-2444**

(Corner of I-80 and N. McCarran, next to Carl's Jr.)

Free use of Self Service Vacuums and Towels!

**rain·x**
Add Rain X Protectant to any Wash for $1.00

MaeAnne
Sierra Highlands
7-11
IHOP
I-80
W. McCarran

facebook **Look for us on Facebook at Jimmys-Express-Carwash-Quick-Lube**

362

# Top Notch Painting

# 20% Off
## Labor Only

Expires December 31, 2011

## Top Notch Painting

In today's tough economy painting remains the simplest, least expensive way to change the look of a room or your home. At Top Notch we provide a wide range of painting services. Whether it's a detailed interior finish or a rental repaint, we pride ourselves on effectively accommodating your needs. We take the "PAIN" out of painting.

- Interior and Exterior Painting
- Offices, Residential, Commercial, Apartments, Rentals & Flips
- Expert Detailed Surface Preparation
- Pressure Washing and Stain Cleaning
- Drywall/Sheetrock Repairs and Texture Matching
- Carpentry and Drywall Repairs
- Wallpaper Removal
- Popcorn (Acoustical) Ceiling Removal
- Color Matching and Decorating

*Licensed and Bonded*
*Over 20 Years Experience*
*References Available Upon Request*

## Call today for your FREE on-site consultation and estimate.
## 775-722-2526

363

**LOCAL'S DISCOUNT GUIDE**

MOTOR CITY MUSIC

"Where Music is Everything"

SPARKS, NEVADA
(775) 331-6366

Big E's Motor City Music
1211 Baring Blvd.
Sparks, NV 89434
In Smith's Shopping Center
331.6366

**LOCAL'S DISCOUNT GUIDE**

# GEMINI
## BALLROOM ACADEMY
*Where your first lesson is always free!*

Gemini Ballroom Academy
2920 Mill Street
Reno, NV 89502
(775) 323-2623
www.geminiballroom.com

**Local's Discount Guide**

**Doggy Day Care and Paw Spa**

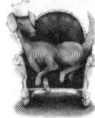

Doggy Day Care and Paw Spa
8995 Double Diamond Suite C-3
Reno, NV 89521
775.825.3647

**Local's Discount Guide**

**Doggy Day Care and Paw Spa**

Doggy Day Care and Paw Spa
8995 Double Diamond Suite C-3
Reno, NV 89521
775.825.3647

**LOCAL'S DISCOUNT GUIDE**

Accurate Mobile Locksmith
P.O. Box 840
Minden, NV 89423
775.265.7444
883.8444

**LOCAL'S DISCOUNT GUIDE**

The Pirate Ship Parties
P.O. Box 60676
Reno, NV 89506
775.636.0922

# SERVICE

*bn*

Ballet Nevada
2910 Mill St.
Reno, NV 89507
329.7026

*Milne* TOWING

Milne Towing
301 Gentry Way
Reno, NV 89502
775.359.0106

*D'Andrea*
*Salon & Spa*

# *D'Andrea Salon & Spa*
# HAIR • SKIN • NAILS
### 30 Years Experience • Gift Certificates Available

## HAIR

- Highlights & Weaves
- Color Specialists
- Color Correction
- Shades EQ

- Specializing in Long Hair, Highlights
- Hair Extensions
- Eyelash Extensions

- Advanced Cutting
- Spiral Perms
- Japanese Permanent Hair Straightening

## SKIN CARE

- Facials
- Full Body Waxing
- Diamond Microdermabrasion
- Chemical Peels
- Permanent Makeup

## NAILS

- Acrylic
- Gels
- Manicures
- Pedicures

## MASSAGES

- Massage Therapy

# 775 • 356 • 7757
### 2965 Vista Blvd., Sparks • Corner of Vista & Baring

Joico • Nexxus • Iso • Paul Mitchell • Dermalogica • Jan Marini • Glycomid

373

## Give The Gift Of Health!

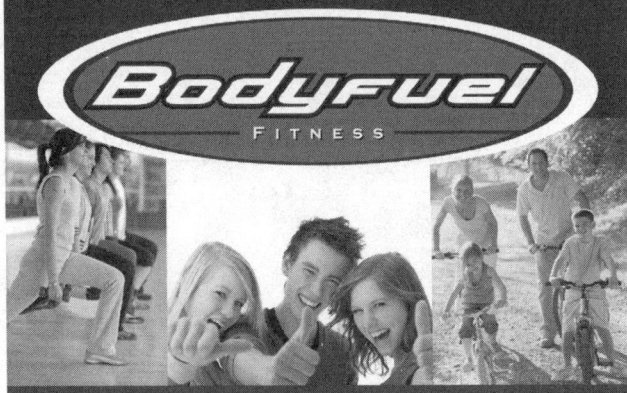

**BodyFuel**
FITNESS

**No** initiation fee
Only **$29.99** a month
for the **ENTIRE FAMILY**
Up to 5 family members maximum
on a shape up membership.

### Enroll Now... Limited Time Offer

### Open 24 Hours A Day*
1264 Disc Drive, Sparks • 775.354.1500

# 15 Days Free
## with this ad
## See club for details.

**BodyFuel**

Expires December 31, 2011

TRANSFORMATION PROMOTION

EXPERIENCE

## AQUARIUS SALON & SPA

FOR YOUR FIRST TIME SERVICE AND RECEIVE

- •50% OFF DESIGN OR COLOR SERVICE
- •30% OFF SKINCARE SERVICE
- •20% OFF NAIL OR WAXING SERVICE

### LIVE IN YOUR TRANSFORMATION

100 N ARLINGTON AVE, SUITE 104, RENO, NV 89501  775-284-8620

TRÉS MICHAEL BENZLEY
MASTER STYLIST / UNITE ARTISTIC DIRECTOR

AQUARIUS SALON & SPA
100 N ARLINGTON AVE, SUITE 104, RENO, NV 89501
775-284-8620

## Aquarius Salon & Spa
## See Above
## For Special Offers

Expires December 31, 2011

# *Bras Plus* **15% Off**
## Total Order

# *Bras Plus*

**1563 So. Virginia, Reno, NV 89502**
**Mon.-Fri. 10-4:00 • Sat 10-3:00**
**(775) 324-3332 • Call for Appointment**

*Specializing in:*
- *Regular Bras 32-56 DD-J*
- *Mastectomy Swimwear & Forms*
- *Breast Prosthesis*
- *Mastectomy Bras*
- *After Surgery Softees*
- *Silicone & Foam Fillers*
- *& More!*

**BEAUTICONTROL.**
BEAUTIFUL SKIN. BEAUTIFUL LIFE.

# TRIM YEARS OFF YOUR APPEARANCE

Instant Face Lifts  ~  Facials  ~  Spa Products

### OPEN HOUSE

Pamper Yourself

### FUN ~ INEXPENSIVE ~ PROVEN

Look younger instantly without risky,
expensive injections or doctor's visits.
BeautiControl is the industry leader
Call for a 10% discount on your first purchase
OR
Tell your friends and earn free products especially for
YOU!

## BeautiControl by Linda G
## (775) 379-6904

# 10% Off
# Total Purchase

**BEAUTICONTROL.**
BEAUTIFUL SKIN. BEAUTIFUL LIFE.

Expires December 31, 2011

# $5 or $10 Off*

*$5 Off a Haircut,
$10 Off a Color or Perm,
$5 Off a Nail Fill, or
$10 Of a Full Set

One coupon per person

## *Charlies*
### HAIR & NAIL DESIGN

Expires December 31, 2011

---

We invite you to become a . . .
Partner in Education.

To become a partner or learn more about the program, contact Coleen DeLong, Partnership Coordinator, Education Alliance at 353-5533 or cdelon@washoe.k12.nv.us. You will be partnered with a school in our district based on the needs of the school and the resources, desire and capacity of your business or service organization. We will arrange and attend a meeting with you and the school principal to get things started. Partnerships can be started at any time.

## education A+ lliance
of Washoe County

* Support Academic Achievement in WCSD
* Provide resources and mentoring to schools and students
* Allow opportunities for your employees to be involved
* Make a positive impact on your community

We invite you to become a...
Partner in Education.

To become a partner or learn more about the program, contact Coleen DeLong, Partnership Coordinator, Education Alliance at 353-5533 or cdelon@washoe.k12.nv.us.
You will be partnered with a school in our district based on the needs of the school and the resources, desire and capacity of your business or service organization. We will arrange and attend a meeting with you and the school principal to get things started. Partnerships can be started at any time.

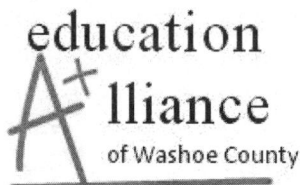

**education**
**A⁺lliance**
of Washoe County

* Support Academic Achievement in WCSD
* Provide resources and mentoring to schools and students
* Allow opportunities for your employees to be involved
* Make a positive impact on your community

LOCAL'S
DISCOUNT
GUIDE

Teased
Hair & Nail
Boutique
358-0503

Teased Hair & Nail Boutique
774 N. McCarran Blvd.
Sparks, NV 89431
358.0503

LOCAL'S
DISCOUNT
GUIDE

element

Element Tanning Studio
3600 Warren Way #105
Reno, NV 89509
775.829.8267

**Ballet Nevada**

# Free Dance Bag

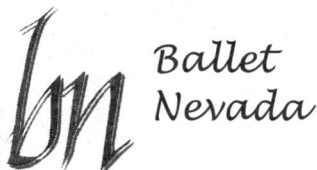

**with paid registration for the year!**
A $25 value. For new students only.
Family registration fee $40/year.
Mention this ad.

Expires December 31, 2011

## *Ballet Nevada LLC*

*We offer classes in Ballet, Jazz, Tap, Tiny Treasures, Boys' Dance, FIT Classes for Teens & Adults & Zumba... for all ages and levels!*

## www.balletnevada.com
## (775) 329-2026

- We offer the best training in Northern Nevada
- We have an outstanding, professional faculty
- We are very family-oriented...
  we care about each and every one of our students
- Community performances throughout the year
- Field Trips to San Francisco Ballet
- Opportunities to compete in the prestigious
  Youth America Grand Prix in San Francisco, CA
- Master Classes & Workshops with
  world-renowned dancers & instructors

2910 Mill Street, Reno, NV 89502 • 775-323-2633

# TRAVEL 15,000 YEARS
## IN JUST A FEW HOURS

## Nevada Historical Society

For more than 10,000 years, people have carved a life here out of the hard, rugged Nevada terrain. From boom to bust, their stories are preserved at the Nevada historical Society in Reno.

Lives and lifestyles of the region's native peoples, first explorers, settlers, miners, ranchers, lawmen,legislators, entertainers, business leaders and those who sought fortune at the hands of Lady Luck unfold in Nevada's oldest state museum. Exhibits detail some of the unmatched technological wonders created to tame this wild land.

**NEVADA HISTORICAL SOCIETY, RENO – 775.688.1190**
1650 North Virginia Street • Reno, Nevada 89503

## NevadaCulture.org

DIVISION OF MUSEUMS AND HISTORY – NEVADA DEPARTMENT OF CULTURAL AFFAIRS            **nevăda**

# GEMINI
## BALLROOM ACADEMY
*Where your first lesson is always free!*

## 3 Private Lessons for $99

**Ballroom - Latin - Swing - Tango - Country - West Coast Swing
Salsa - Social Dancing
Call today to book your first FREE Private Lesson!**

Expires December 31, 2011

# GEMINI
# BALLROOM ACADEMY
## Where your first lesson is always free!

# 775-323-2623

At Gemini Ballroom, we strive to create a fun and easy going atmosphere that makes learning to dance a variety of dances fast, fun and easy!

We offer private lessons, group classes and practice sessions to teens and adults in all Ballroom, Latin, Swing, Salsa, Country and Social Dance styles.

Become our fan on Facebook
Visit us online at www.GeminiBallroom.com

# Silver State
# Peace Officers Museum
## A National Collection

Step Back in Time!

Silver State Peace Officers Museum
Virginia City, Nevada

# 26 South B Street
# Virginia City, Nevada
### Inside the historic 1876 Jail and Courthouse!

# www.PeaceOfficersMuseum.org

We invite you to become a . . .
Partner in Education.

To become a partner or learn more about the program, contact Coleen DeLong, Partnership Coordinator, Education Alliance at 353-5533 or cdelon@washoe.k12.nv.us.
You will be partnered with a school in our district based on the needs of the school and the resources, desire and capacity of your business or service organization. We will arrange and attend a meeting with you and the school principal to get things started. Partnerships can be started at any time.

# education
# A⁺lliance
## of Washoe County

* Support Academic Achievement in WCSD
* Provide resources and mentoring to schools and students
* Allow opportunities for your employees to be involved
* Make a positive impact on your community

ROMERO
DESIGNS

Personalized and Photo Jewelry
in sterling silver and 14 carat gold

Introducing Our New Collection
www.romerodesigns.com

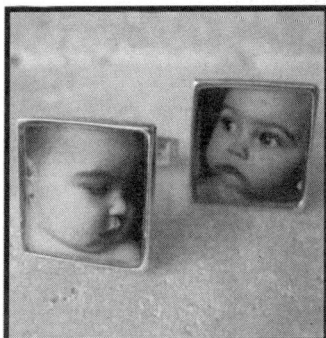

15% off all pieces through The Locals Discount Guide
tami@romerodesigns.com • 203.531.5265

Expires December 31, 2011

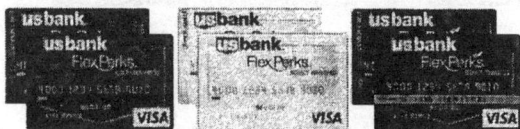